A Brief Theology of Sport

With lively prose, conceptual clarity and a deep affection for the subject matter, Harvey kicks off an important conversation about how theologically we should make sense of – and order our love in relation to – a central cultural phenomenon of our times: sport. Wonderfully insightful, historically rich and theologically punchy, this is vital reading for anyone who plays, watches or is utterly bemused by the world of sport.

Luke Bretherton
Associate Professor of Theological Ethics and Senior Fellow at the Kenan
Institute for Ethics
Duke University, USA

Dr Lincoln Harvey has managed to do something quite remarkable here: this book is at once historical and constructive; academic and accessible; detailed and concise; systematic and practical. It is good to see serious work done on theology and sport, and this book is a fine example of what serious theology about contemporary issues should look like.

Tom Greggs
Professor of Historical and Doctrinal Theology
Aberdeen University, UK

Lincoln Harvey is a soccer fan, and one of the most besotted sort, a supporter of Arsenal. What as a Christian should he make of the hours spent absorbed in an activity that does nothing but itself? I give away only a hint of his profound proposal by citing a chapter title: "A Liturgical Celebration of Contingency". This is high flying theology that manages to be a good read – not a common achievement.

Robert W. Jenson,
Formerly Senior Scholar for Research at the Center of Theological Inquiry,
Princeton, USA
Professor Emeritus of Religion, St. Olaf College, Minnesota, USA

This is a brilliant book. Brief but profound, brimming full of ideas and intriguing insights, it achieves something rare and yet deeply satisfying for those of us who love both God and sport – relating them to each other in a way that does proper justice to both.

Graham Tomlin,
Dean, St Mellitus College, London, UK

LINCOLN HARVEY

A Brief Theology
of Sport

scm press

© Lincoln Harvey 2014

Published in 2014 by SCM Press
Editorial office
3rd Floor
Invicta House
108–114 Golden Lane
London
EC1Y 0TG

SCM Press is an imprint of Hymns Ancient & Modern Ltd
(a registered charity)
13A Hellesdon Park Road
Norwich NR6 5DR, UK

www.scmpress.co.uk

British Library Cataloguing in Publication data

A catalogue record for this book is available
from the British Library

978-0-334-04418-5

Typeset by Manila Typesetting Company
Printed and bound by
CPI Group (UK) Ltd

Contents

Introduction

A Question of Sport

I love it when Arsenal play at home. Last Saturday was no exception. First, I met my friends in a local pub. The starting line-up was discussed, the opposition reviewed and the tempting odds on victory confidently embraced. Then soon enough, like agitated atoms in a cyclonic swirl, we left the pub to join the 60,000 other fans making their way to the ground. Amid the colourful sea of hats, scarves and replica shirts, we marched under a railway tunnel – cue echoing chant, 'Red Army, Red Army' – and past programme sellers, fanzine sellers and all sorts of merchandise, before finally reaching the densely packed bottleneck: security, stewards, slow clunking turnstiles, and then at last inside: the bright dazzling pitch, the titanic noise, the players emerging, the volume increasing, the whistle blowing, the match kicking off. Football, I love it.

To be honest, the game was nothing special. A dour opposition attempted to crush our creativity to protect their scoreless draw through the regimented process of sterile hoofing, persistent fouling and the strategic wasting of valuable time. Nevertheless, the game still worked its magic. Time and space went all funny, the intensity of life somehow compressed into 90 minutes, stretched across an emerald pitch, as I was strung between a moment all anxious and tensed, miles from my worries, miles from my cares, the immediacy of the game somehow gripping me, absorbing me, with all its twists and turns, swift darting movements and subtle fleeting passes that merge and break, undetermined and free as the game suddenly explodes: Alex Song to Van Persie who volleys . . . ONE NIL . . . and we all go ballistic, leaping and hollering, bouncing and shouting,

vii

punching the air in the purest delight. Football, there is nothing quite like it.[1]

The game ended soon enough, and I was transported – crushed onto a Tube train – back into the pressurized space of every-day life. But while the 22 players changed into designer clothes before climbing into splendid cars to drive off towards mag-nificent mansions, I found myself wondering what it was I had witnessed. Nothing had been produced. Nothing had been har-vested. The game had simply begun and it had simply ended. It was a passing event that left no mark on the world in which we live. Of course, Arsenal had won three more points. But these three points – to be celebrated nonetheless – held no real value beyond the self-contained universe of the league in which we play. I also knew the players had become richer, while my friends and I had grown somewhat poorer, but the professional game's perverted finances are not its purpose; money is secondary, aux-iliary at best. And so it was – squashed inside a train carriage – that a nihilistic wave washed over me: the game is pointless; it is for nothing, it holds no purpose. Yet, for some strange reason, this knowledge did not bother me. In fact, it made me feel even better. Football, it really is a funny old game.

II

Arsenal play their football in the English Premier League. The league runs from August through to May each year. It is made up of 20 professional clubs, which are drawn from towns and cities across the length and breadth of England.[2] Every year each team plays the other teams twice, both home and away, with points being allocated in line with results, each result determined by the scoring of goals and each goal scored though a complex mix of skill, mistakes and random chance. By the end of the season, the team that has the most points is crowned champions (unless, if points are tied, goal difference settles it).

The Premier League is incredibly popular. A vast number of fans now watch it, as well as a growing company of corporate spectators whose unwanted presence epitomizes the unsociability of corporate extravagance. This year for example, during the 2011–12 season, over 13 million tickets were sold for the 380 games, a startling figure which produces an average crowd of around 35,000 per game.[3] Given the finite number of seats available, this figure constitutes something of a sell-out, with the imperial laws of supply and demand making match-day tickets pricey and quite difficult to get hold of. At Arsenal, for instance, the cheapest season ticket now costs a fraction under a thousand pounds. Despite this financial hurdle, people still queue up to pay. Whatever its shortcomings, the English Premier League is clearly popular.[4]

There are many ways to explain the popularity of the Premier League. For example, the games are endlessly promoted through mainstream (and niche) media outlets, with aggressive marketing and constant self-aggrandizement.[5] But behind the glamour and glitz of the marketing gimmicks, the underlying reason for the league's popularity should not be overlooked. The Premier League is popular, because football is popular.

This simple equation explains why there are over 37,000 football teams here in England. Some of these teams are on the fringe of the Premiership, making up the second, third and fourth tiers of the professional game. But the overwhelming majority of these teams are amateur, performing Saturday-by-Saturday and Sunday-by-Sunday in parks and pitches across the land. The Football Association – the game's governing body in England – estimates that over 7 million people play the game on a regular basis in this country. That is 4 million children and 3 million adults. Given that the population of England – including the elderly, infirm and babes-in-arms – is around 51 million, 7 million is a sizeable chunk. It means that around one in seven people are playing football on a regular basis in England. A simple hypothesis suggests itself: the English love football.[6]

Of course, the English are not alone. Football – or soccer as it is elsewhere known – is the most popular sport in the world, something demonstrated every four years when the FIFA World Cup is held. Over 200 countries compete for a place in this month-long tournament, a process that culminates in the World Cup Final where two teams contend for the famous gold trophy. This particular match is broadcast live to over two hundred countries, with over a billion people watching the game unfold on television. It has been estimated that over 90 per cent of the world's television-owning households tune into the final.[7] This shows that football's popularity is global. But what makes this particular game so popular?

When we think about it the answer is not obvious. Stripped of its razzamatazz, investment and hyped-up emotion – boiled down to its essential parts, as it were – the World Cup Final is little more than 22 men in competitive concert trying to advance a bright spherical object (historically, a pig's bladder no less) across manicured grass and over a thin white line painted between two upright posts, crossed with a bar and from which hangs a net. That is it. Nothing else. So why would a billion people tune in to this event?[8]

And football is not alone. We could just as easily be talking about a whole host of different sports. Half the American people watch the annual Super Bowl, for instance, where two armour-plated teams fearlessly advance an egg-shaped ball in pursuit of a 'touchdown', while millions of others enjoy the peculiarity of NBA basketball where the trajectory of a bouncing ball is directed towards a raised, backed hoop. And there are baseball fans, golf fans, tennis fans and cricket fans. The list is almost endless. It is not just football people love. It is *sport*. But the question remains: *why do people love it?*[9]

If things were a little different – contrary to fact – this question would be much easier to answer. Imagine if everyone was tuning in to watch the best farmers plough, the best builders build or the best doctors operate. If this were the case, we could quickly conclude that these activities are vitally important to us. Agriculture provides the food which keeps us alive. Architecture provides the buildings which shelter us. And healthcare provides the remedies which rescue people from pain and disease. So of course we want to celebrate the best practitioners in these arts. If we were to think of it, the Ploughing World Cup – or some such variant – makes perfect sense. But that is not the tournament we watch. It is football that we love.[10]

This imaginary scenario could encourage us to draw a straight line between survival and sport. Just as farming, housing and healthcare are linked to survival, maybe sport is too? Physical prowess, for instance, could be linked to our preparation for battle, meaning – as George Orwell once put it – that modern sport is simply 'war without the guns', something that satisfies the displaced violence still latent in us all.[11] Or we might instead see things differently, sensing that sport is a fossilized residue from some ancient rituals in which our ancestors petitioned the gods, seeking their blessings in life so that they might survive amid threat and fear. To mutate Orwell, maybe sport is simply religion without the sacrifice?[12] But joining up the dots in these ways would be a mistake. Though both answers – war and religion – are nearly right, they are also very much wrong. They are in fact looking in the right place, but in the wrong sort of way. Sport has everything to do with our deepest identity, but it is an identity much more basic than the corrupted desire to survive through either violent battle or religious bartering. Sport is to do with our true nature. It is to do with who we really are. It is a question of our created *being*.

III

This book will help us understand our love for sport through an account of our most basic identity as creatures. The account offered – like any explanation – will require us to look at sport from a particular angle. This is not to say that the argument is written from the viewpoint of an Arsenal fan, though it is. It is instead to recognize that the book is written from the perspective of a Christian. This is a *Christian* theology of sport.

Nowadays, as so often in the past, most people do not want to look at things from a Christian perspective. They think that Christian explanations are riddled with superstitious nonsense, far-fetched myths and imaginary beings. This renders Christian explanations at best redundant and at worst dangerous in an increasingly atheistic culture that listens only to the crisp voice of objectivity intoned with demonstrable evidence and spoken in tune with scientific reasoning. This modern prejudice against Christian speech is undoubtedly unfair. Objectivity, demonstrable evidence and rationality – just like the Christian faith – are inescapably local. There is no view-from-nowhere, no tradition-less perspective. Every explanation, however much we disguise it, comes from within a community of faith. Fortunately, the modern fetish for 'faithless' forms of arguing has itself now fallen under suspicion, and, with its vice-like grip weakening, alternative voices can again be heard. In this changing climate (not without its own risks), Christians are again speaking with confidence. They are making their case on the faithful foundation of the good news that Jesus Christ is Lord. As a result, we will be looking at sport from a Christian perspective unashamedly, with confidence.[13]

But, in approaching the question theologically, we beat a (relatively) untrodden path. This is not to ignore the recent flurry of activity here in the UK, much of which was fuelled by the London Olympics in 2012 and a desire to make hay while the sun shines. On the whole, however, Christian theologians have not focused their minds on the question of sport. A glance through the colourful catalogues of theological publishers – as well as the index of recent works in systematic theology – quickly establishes the fact. There is next to no reference to sport.[14] This gap might suggest that theologians are not that interested in sport, there being some mysterious relation between the intellectual life and sporting endeavour, with embryonic academics preferring a book in the hand over a ball at their feet. This may explain why academics are quite happy to explore all sorts of social, political and cultural phenomena – especially those from (self-designated) high culture – while managing to avoid the question of sport altogether.[15] Alternatively, theologians may be avoiding the question of sport because thinking about it runs the risk of confusing their hobby with their work and thereby blurs the boundaries between their leisure and career. Whatever the reason(s), the simple point remains: a review of the literature finds little evidence of theological engagement with the question of sport.

Given sport's popularity, this oversight should strike us as odd. But with its oddity noted, it is important to recognize that a good number of Christian thinkers are wrestling with issues in sport. Many authors have focused on questions surrounding faith and performance – does saying your prayers make you run faster? – or have instead tackled the ethical quandaries that spring from the clashing cultures of Christian nice-ness and the competitive spirit.[16] Such works are important. But they do not constitute a theology of sport per se. Theology neat, so to speak, asks more fundamental questions, enquiring into the very nature of the object – what it *is* – rather than setting out on the assumption that the object is known and can be examined in relation to a second known object, in this case Christianity. Things are less certain for the theologian. Theologians attempt to give voice to reality by speaking in tune with the event of God's own self-introduction in Jesus Christ. It is gospel-shaped speech, and it is no easy task.

The difficulty of the task must not become an excuse, however. Christian theologians must attempt to speak with God and their neighbours on the basis of the gospel. This book takes up this challenge. It is an attempt to explore the ways of God with creation in Jesus Christ, and – through the Church's understanding of those ways – to discover what it is that makes sport so popular today.[17]

The argument – mercifully – is quite simple. The reader will be guided through various doctrines as we unpack the theological components of the argument step by step, spelling out the relevant implications and underscoring the value of a Christian understanding of reality for a proper appreciation of sport. This patient approach means that the reader need not have studied theology formally before. The book is instead written in a way that will allow a wide range of people – both inside and outside the Church – to understand their passion for sport in light of the gospel of Jesus Christ. To that end, all the reader will need is an enquiring mind and a sustaining interest.

This step-by-step approach could alienate the specialist reader, especially those who possess a firm grasp of the Church's teachings on God's act of creation. I can only ask such readers to be patient. I do believe their patience will be rewarded, however, because the argument of the book constitutes an original contribution to public discourse, one that manages to harness the Church's historical approach to sport while driving it in a new direction. This is a genuinely constructive proposal, which invites everyone to re-imagine sport.

The structure of the book is also simple, though it falls into two parts. In the first part, we will take some historical soundings. These soundings will help us understand the ways in which Christians have engaged with sport in the past. That said, history in the plain sense is not the foundation on which the proposal rests. That foundation lies elsewhere. It is *theological*, the story of God with his creatures. But it is important for us to begin with history. Before we say anything remotely constructive, we need to listen to those who have gone before us. This will give us a sense of the context into which we speak.

That being said, however, we are not going to labour excessively over the archaeological evidence or catalogue the encyclopaedic details in this book. Other books serve that purpose well.[18] Instead, we will look only to trace the lie of the land, capturing – in summary – the overall shape of the historical relation between religion and sport. Though this approach is risky – history is much messier than the lessons we draw from it! – it will allow us to bring the rudimentary question more sharply into focus: should Christians be involved in sports at all?

To that end, we will first highlight the close relationship between ancient sports and ancient religions, before turning to examine classical sports in Greece and Rome. These initial excavations will set the scene, allowing us to see the way in which sport and religion always intertwine and interconnect. Only then – in the third chapter – will we begin to examine how Christians have approached sport, identifying a two-fold approach of opposition and instrumental use in the early Church. With this twofold pattern in mind, we will then briefly examine two further case studies – in the fourth and fifth chapters – to see if the early pattern repeats. In these two chapters, we will first look at the medieval Church and its approach to the jousts and tournaments, before turning to look at Protestant approaches to sport, notably that of the Puritans and Muscular Christians. These short case studies will demonstrate how easily sport turns into a rival form of religion, one that mistakenly idolizes natural power, physical guile and the brutish ways of fallen creatures and thereby tempts Christians on to alternative paths of discipleship that take them away from their Lord. We will therefore conclude that history regularly poses Christians a serious question: sport *or* a life of discipleship?

The stark nature of this choice will baffle many of us today. It is now too easy to celebrate a love of sport *and* a faith in Jesus Christ, with some people even going so far as to see sport as a form of worship, a positive exercise of body and spirit that enables the players to merge with the Now in the energy of flow as they delightfully commune with their Maker.[19] In fact, blind celebration of sport is more common today than debilitating suspicion. Nonetheless, I will argue that neither blind celebration nor debilitating suspicion is the right approach for the Christian. Instead, Christians need to steer a careful route between these two extremes, harnessing the moment of truth in each but avoiding the mistakes along the way. In so doing, we will be able to celebrate sport for what it is without confusing it for what it isn't.

To that end, we will begin to analyse sport more closely in the second half of the book. In Chapter 6, we will draw on conversations in the philosophy of play to develop a working definition of sport, something that we can then analyse further through an exploration of the teachings of the Church about the divine act of creation in Chapter 7. This move into doctrine will allow us to discover a clear rationale for the popularity of sport by seeing how it is linked to the Christian understanding of the very *being* of the creature. This theological rationale will provide us with the conceptual tools to argue in Chapter 8 that sport is the place where the human creature chimes with its own being in the delightful knowledge that it is neither God nor nothing. In effect, we will propose that sport is the ritual celebration of our contingency, a liturgy of our meaningful non-necessity that should not be confused with an act of worship. Worship celebrates who God is. Sport celebrates who we are. It is our liturgical celebration of our graced selves.

On the basis of this dogmatic proposal, the final two chapters of the book will constitute a call to Christians to re-appraise their approach to sport. Having examined topics such as rules, competition, gender, and good and bad sports, we will argue that Christians should move beyond traditional opposition and instrumental use and instead adopt a posture of non-instrumental celebration (while cautioning against idolatry). In short, the Church needs to celebrate sport as an appropriate feature of a truly Sabbath-shaped life. The future need not repeat the past. It is time for change.

The book therefore works in two parts. The first part is historical. The second part is dogmatic. These two parts work together, though the dogmatic section has priority. In effect, the historical section will not make sense without subsequent theological analysis, because doctrine is concerned with the primary history of God-with-his-creatures by which alone we can really understand what is happening in our world. However, any reader who is already familiar with the historical relationship between sport and religion can skip to the second part of the book, pursuing the theological analysis offered there. In effect, the analytic section is self-standing; the historical one is not.

The book also operates on two levels, the specialist and non-specialist. This means in practice that it can be read straight through or instead be punctuated with regular detours into the thicket of endnotes. Readers can rest assured that the constructive argument stands entirely in the main body of the text. The endnotes simply supplement the argument by steering specialist readers towards points of detail or avenues for further reading, or instead acknowledge the many shoulders I am standing on. If a reader therefore decides to skip the endnotes, he or she will miss nothing of importance in the constructive argument. In fact, most readers will find that the endnotes break the argument's flow. As a result, the endnotes should be handled with care.

Despite the confidence with which the book is written, I offer only a tentative proposal here. The account – both in its historical investigations and dogmatic enquiries – is largely episodic and impressionistic and is far from being the last word on the subject. It is written instead as a conversation starter, providing a doctrinal framework for Christians to discuss how sport should fit within a life of discipleship. The argument has itself been shaped by a number of important conversations, for all of which I am grateful. I have benefited from the constructive criticism of friends, colleagues and strangers, who in their different ways have made the argument much stronger than it would have been if I had been left to my own devices. I am especially grateful to Alan Spence, Terry J. Wright and Christopher C. Roberts for reading through various drafts of the book and for making constructive criticisms along the way, as well as to those who have been diligently praying for the project in the background. I have also benefited from comments made on various versions of the argument in seminars and conferences at King's College London, Regent's Park College, Oxford, the University of Gloucester, the School of Theology in Sheffield and the Work in Progress seminar at Westminster Abbey. I am also grateful for the kind permission of the editors to make use of material from my earlier work in *Anvil* 28.1 (2012) and *The International Journal of Religion and Sport* 2 (2013).

I am also thankful for the consistent support of my various colleagues at St Mellitus College, not least our Dean, Graham Tomlin, whose advice and encouragement for this long-running project has been unwavering and welcome, as has that of Stephen Backhouse and Chris Tilling. I have also been extremely lucky to enjoy the support of Natalie Watson at SCM Press, who has managed the project with remarkable patience and good will, enduring my many failings and gracefully accommodating my slow progress and revised deadlines. I want to thank Dominic Ahearne, Eddie Bovingdon, Gary Cullen, Michael Nicholas and Steven Nicholas for helping me put the theory into practice, and also my mum and my dad for their constant encouragement. I thank Tereza for her unfailing love (and for understanding why I must go to Arsenal every other week!) and Anna and Georgia for being so brilliant. Finally, this book is dedicated to Rose Harvey, my daughter. In her short time with us, Rose has taught me more than anyone else that life is not that serious, but that its meaning is love.

Notes

1 As will be clear to some readers, this chapter was written while Robin Van Persie and Alex Song still played for Arsenal. Sadly, loyalty in football is a virtue found primarily in fans. Therefore, I was tempted to update the narrative to include current players, but suspect that this would only prove a temporary reprieve. Therefore, I have stuck with the original text, dated though it is. For an interesting discussion about the involvement of fans as participants in sport, see Michael Novak, *The Joy of Sports: Endzones, Bases, Baskets, Balls, and the Consecration of the American Spirit*, rev. edn, Lanham, ML: Madison, 1994, p. 24.

2 Somewhat unusually, the league currently includes two teams from Wales (Swansea City and Cardiff City). The precise make-up of the league changes each year through the merry-go-round of relegation and promotion.

3 For details and a range of statistics, see the *Premier League Season Review* 2011–12, available at http://addison.ceros.com/premier-league/season-review-2011-12/page/1.

4 Strangely, despite its popularity, the Premier League is simultaneously unpopular, with many questioning the way in which the game has become dominated by money since its introduction. For an important review of wider issues surrounding the commercialization of modern sport, see Paul Bickley and Sam Tomlin, *Give Us Our Ball Back: Reclaiming Sport for the Common Good*, London: Theos, 2012.

5 For an excellent – and funny – review of the relationship between sport and television, see Martin Kelner, *Sit Down and Cheer: A History of Sport on TV*, Guildford: John Wisden and Company, 2012.

6 The figures are taken from the English Football Association: http://www.thefa.com/TheFA/WhoWeAre.aspx. Note: one in seven people *currently* play.

Many non-players will be former players who no longer play due to old age or bad health. Without doubt, football is a very popular sport.

7 According to FIFA's figures, the World Cup Finals of 1998, 2002 and 2006 attracted global audiences of 1.3 billion, 1.1 billion and 715 million people respectively. Initiative Sports Futures conclude that the 2006 Final was watched by 260 million in the 54 key markets it surveyed, accounting for 90 per cent of the world's TV households. ISF figures come from data collated electronically by reputable monitors, such as Barb in the UK. 'Why FIFA's claim of one billion TV viewers was a quarter right', *Independent*, 1 March 2007. Though, we should note, the television audience is in some sense 'soft' – with 'soft' being a technical term used to highlight the fact that people might watch for negative reasons (for example, lousy weather or the lack of decent programmes on alternative channels). See Garry Whannel, 'Sport and the Media', in Jay Coakley and Eric Dunning (eds), *Handbook of Sports Studies*, London: Sage, 2002, p. 293. For a brief discussion of sport's global popularity from a Christian perspective, see Pete Wilcox, 'Glory', in Samuel Wells and Sarah Coakley (eds), *Praying for England: Priestly Presence in Contemporary Culture*, London and New York: Continuum, 2008, pp. 41–64.

8 We should be wary of this kind of rhetorical reductionism: 'to think of football as merely 22 hirelings kicking a ball is to say that a violin is merely wood and cat-gut, Hamlet is so much ink and paper . . .', J. B. Priestley, cited in Wilcox, 'Glory', p. 43.

9 In the UK, football is the most popular sport among many other popular sports. See the estimated numbers of people playing different sports at http://www.sportengland.org/research/active_people_survey/active_people_survey_3.aspx. Of course, people can love more than one sport, so the numbers need to take that into account.

10 I have seen signs – in the English countryside – for forthcoming Ploughing Matches. However, these are local events which do not attract a global television audience, so the point remains. That said, though we are yet to see the equivalent of the Ploughing World Cup, we should also note that British television is awash with programmes about competitive chefs, e.g. *Cup Cake Wars*, *Great British Bake Off*, *Masterchef*.

11 George Orwell, 'The Sporting Spirit', *Tribune* (14 December 1945). For a brief discussion of Orwell's views on sport, see Nigel Spivey, *The Ancient Olympics*, 2nd edn, Oxford: Oxford University Press, 2012, pp. 1–4.

12 For a helpful discussion of the religious nature of modern sports, see Robert J. Higgs and Michael C. Braswell, *An Unholy Alliance: The Sacred and Modern Sport*, Macon, GA: Mercer University Press, 2004.

13 Make no mistake, Christian explanations *are* rational. It is simply that Christian rationality is irreducibly *theological*. For a good introduction to methodological issues in contemporary discourse, see William C. Placher, *Unapologetic Theology: A Christian Voice in a Pluralist Conversation*, Louisville, KY: Westminster John Knox Press, 1989. For an attempt to understand the reasons behind the opposition to Christian scholarship, see George M. Marsden, *The Outrageous Idea of Christian Scholarship*, Oxford and New York: Oxford University Press, 1997. Richard J. Bernstein helpfully summarizes the current

state of play: '[T]he basic conviction is that when we turn to the examination of those concepts that philosophers have taken to be most fundamental – whether it is the concept of rationality, truth, reality, right, the good, or norms – we are forced to recognize that in the final analysis all such concepts must be understood as relative to a specific conceptual scheme, theoretical framework, paradigm, form of life, society or culture . . . It is an illusion to think that there is something that might properly be labelled "*the* standards of rationality", standards that are genuinely universal and that are not subject to historical or temporal change.' Richard J. Bernstein, *Beyond Objectivism and Relativism: Science, Hermeneutics, and Praxis*, Oxford: Basil Blackwell, 1983, p. 8.

14 The lack of material is regularly lamented in print. For example, Robert K. Johnston recognizes that there is 'little or no serious theological reflection currently focussing on our play.' Robert K. Johnston, *The Christian at Play*, Grand Rapids, MI: Eerdmans, 1997, p. ix. William J. Baker argues that 'evangelicals have yet to produce anything approximating a theology of sport'. William J. Baker, *Playing with God: Religion and Modern Sport*, Cambridge, MA: Harvard University Press, 2007, p. 217. Anderson and Marino also note, 'Despite the long co-evolution of sport and religion, there have been few academic venues open to the discussion of their intricate interrelationship.' Christopher J. Anderson and Gordon Marino (eds), *International Journal of Religion and Sport* 1 (2009), editors' page. Nick Watson in a review concludes that 'scholars from theology and religious studies have failed to take sport seriously, for it is arguably the West's most popular cultural pastime now, surpassing other previously dominant cultural expressions such as music and art'. Nick Watson, 'Book Review: *An Unholy Alliance: The Sacred and Modern Sports* by Robert J. Higgs and Michael C. Braswell, 2004', *Implicit Religion* 10.3 (2007), pp. 314–16. That being said, sport – as we shall see in Chapter 6 – has held the attention of a number of philosophers over recent years. See, for example, H. J. Vander Zwaag, *Toward a Philosophy of Sport*, Fort Worth: University of Texas Press, 1985; Drew Hyland, *A Philosophy of Sport*, Lanham: University Press of America, 1990; and Steven Conner, *A Philosophy of Sport*, London: Reaktion Books, 2011, among many.

15 'The *intellectual* thing, the *liberal* thing, the *mature* thing is to set sports aside.' Novak, *The Joy of Sports*, p. xvii.

16 Shirl Hoffman's subtitle, 'Can the mind of Christ coexist with the killer instinct?', helpfully sums up the issue. Shirl J. Hoffman, 'The Sanctification of Sport', *Christianity Today* 30.6 (1986), p. 18, cited in Stuart Weir, 'Competition as Relationship: Sport as a Mutual Quest Towards Excellence', in Donald Deedorff and John White (eds), *The Image of God in the Human Body: Essays on Christianity and Sports*, New York: Edwin Mellen, 2008. For a popular exploration of the ethical conundrums facing Christians in sports, see Ted Kluck, *The Reason for Sports: A Christian Fanifesto*, Chicago IL: Moody Publishers, 2009. For a much more academic approach to the question of prayer and performance, see Nick J. Watson and Daniel R. Czech, 'The Use of Prayer in Sport: Implications for Sport Pyschology Consulting', *Athletic Insight* 7.4 (2005), pp. 26–35. For a systematic review of the literature in this field, see Nick J. Watson and Andrew Parker, 'Sports and Christianity: Mapping the Field',

in Nick J. Watson and Andrew Parker (eds), *Sports and Christianity: Historical Contemporary Perspectives*, New York and Abingdon: Routledge, 2013, pp. 9–88.

17 A word or two on issues surrounding the capitalizing of the word *Church*: the use of the capital denotes my attempt to speak of the Church as a whole, through time, the Church universal. This can imply that the Church *has* certain characteristics or, importantly, *should* have them. Such usage will raise all sorts of questions about Christian identity for readers, who will inevitably question my employment of 'Church' in places. My use of it should not become a stumbling block, however, as the argument does not depend on it.

18 For an example of an encyclopaedic history of sport (though without a focus on religion), see Martin Polley (ed.), *The History of Sport in Britain, 1880–1914*, London: Routledge, 2003.

19 For example, Bryan Mason writes: 'We must destroy the perception that sport and physical education are "below the line" and fit into the unspiritual category. In God's economy there is no sacred–secular divide. In the words of the Westminster catechism we are "to love God and enjoy him forever" and this can be fulfilled as effectively on the sports field as it can inside a church.' Bryan Mason, *The Teaching of Physical Education: A Biblical Perspective* (The Christian Institute, 2002), based on a lecture given at St Stephen's Church Centre, Newcastle upon Tyne, on 23 May 2002, available at http://www.christian.org.uk/html-publications/education9.htm.

PART I

Historical Soundings

I

Ancient Sports and Religion

A question for the first part of the book: *how has the Church engaged with sports?*

If we take the meandering course of history as a whole, we discover that the Church has – thus far – struggled to celebrate sport. In fact, the opposite is more often the case. Though particular sports are from time to time used as part of the evangelistic strategy of local churches, sport has seldom been celebrated in and of itself. Instead, sport has been viewed with suspicion. This is because the Church thinks sport is inextricably caught up in the idolatrous worship of false gods. It is linked to the pagan celebration of the power of nature simply in and of itself. Therefore ecclesial history – again, thus far – confronts the Christian with a challenge. Is it possible to reconcile the gospel with a love for sport or must Christians recognize that sport has no place in the Christian life?

This stark choice will strike many people as odd today. That is because we will know – or ourselves be – the type of Christian who embraces the life of faith while fully participating in the world of sport. It is therefore quite hard for modern Christians to imagine how playing ice hockey could undermine their love for Jesus, or an enjoyment of baseball be opposed to a lively faith. Of course, we will all know there are times when the Christian's love for sport will clash with the life of discipleship, with Sundays often proving a crunch point. Sports fans regularly have to choose between going to church and attending a game; loyalties can be torn. But in this day and age, Christians are pretty good at getting the two worlds to run in parallel. As a result, a lot of Christians will find it difficult to imagine how an afternoon on the golf course can impact their devotion to Jesus Christ. Kept far enough apart, sport and faith can live happily together.

This is not to say that Christians will not have doubts niggling away at the back of their minds. They will have questions to do with brutal competition and the radical call to forgiving charity. How can someone love their neighbour while at the same time pursue victory over them? But this tricky question – important though it is – is a million miles from the stark question raised by history. Is sport fundamentally incompatible with the Christian faith?

To understand where this question comes from – and its pressing nature – we need to recognize that religion has always been woven into sport, and vice versa. If we dig down a little, we soon discover that ancient sporting tournaments were held in temples and plenty of altars have been placed in stands, with the rules and regulations of sporting contests often being determined by cultic myths about the supernatural ordering of the universe. This will also sound strange to some Christians today. It is hard to imagine what football – for example – has to do with the harmonious ordering of the universe (even if we do sense the quasi-religious nature of contemporary fandom). For many, the religious life finds its expression *away* from the sports field and is not expressed through it. In fact, religion is often over-spiritualized today, with the body becoming an obstacle to the pursuit of mystical experience. Think only of the popular flight through the navel, achieved through the stilling and transcending of the body and entry into the abstracted stillness of a Zen-like state. These contemporary forms of Gnosticism – an ancient esoteric sect, distrustful of matter – seek to escape embodiment by accessing a superior spiritual realm. Whatever cosmic force the practitioner dissolves into, it is rarely celebrated for its dynamic physicality.

That said, the compartmentalization of the Christian life – where trips to watch Arsenal are irrelevant to life at the altar! – is often this Gnostic mistake moved only a notch. But history teaches us something quite different. Usually, sport and religion are not separated. History instead muddies the two. The burden of this chapter is to justify this claim.

II

A proposition with which to begin: *neither local nor new, sport is universal.*

In many respects, our first proposition is not true. Sports can be local. Americans enjoy baseball, the Irish enjoy hurling, and the game of cricket piggybacked on the sprawling British Empire. Likewise, sports can be new. Skateboarding, snowboarding and synchronized swimming – to name but obvious examples – have only recently emerged, while sports such as Indy Car racing, speedway and waterskiing have relied on technological developments in motorized transport. Nevertheless, it remains true to say that sport is neither local nor new. This is because sport has been played always and everywhere.[1]

Consider North America. Today, Americans love sport. American football, baseball and basketball are the most popular, drawing in their legions of fans from across the land. But sport stretches not only across American terrain; it also stretches back in American time. When the first European settlers arrived at the end of the fifteenth century, they discovered that the indigenous peoples were already playing sport. The local people were enjoying competitive archery, javelin and racing contests, as well as more exotic-sounding games like 'snow snake' (in which darts were glided across a frozen lake) and 'stickball' (a forerunner to the modern sport of lacrosse).[2] Stickball was known by many names, among which stand out 'little war' (*da-nah-wah'uwsdi*), 'little brother of war' (*Tewaarathon*), 'bump hips' (*baaga'adowe*), and 'men hit rounded object' (*dehuntshigwa'es*). As these descriptive names suggest, stickball was a war-like game involving a stick-like instrument. It was played with two teams – often neighbouring tribes – with the number of players ranging anywhere from a dozen through into the hundreds. The duration of the game was also variable, sometimes hours, sometimes days, with the playing area ranging from 100 feet to several miles in length. The basic game, however, was consistent in shape. Two goals were set up, using either a natural object (perhaps a rock or a tree) or something tailored for the job (a long pole, up to eight metres in height, tipped with intricate carvings of fishes, birds or animals). Players would then hit a ball towards the target, with points being awarded for a direct strike. Beyond this, however, little was ruled out and little ruled in. Tackling therefore featured strongly – bump hips! – with the resulting free-for-all involving violent off-the-ball wrestling. The game was often reduced to little more than a sprawling melee of writhing bodies. As one of its names suggests, this ancient sport really did look like a 'little brother of war'.

Africa's story is similar to America's.[3] Sport has been played everywhere, always. In the Sudan, for example, before Western colonists arrived, entire villages would gather for community wrestling tournaments. The Nuba tribe – to take a well-studied example – would begin their tournaments with dramatic rituals, first covering the wrestlers in ghostly ash to prepare their entrance into the borderlands of death. Once ashed in this way, the wrestlers were adorned with long woven tails (thought to symbolize the cattle on which the tribe depended, a connection further emphasized by the bellowing roars and stamping of feet that dominated proceedings). Thus prepared, the contestants would adopt a sumo-like pose, roaring wildly and then suddenly striking, pulling, grappling and drawing their opponent down into the dust.[4]

Likewise in India:[5] ancient texts such as the *Ramayana* (composed between 500 and 300 BC) and the *Mahabharata* (authored between 400 BC and AD 400) show that sporting tournaments were held over 3,000 years ago, with the same being true in China. Cuju – now recognized to be the distant ancestor of football – can be traced back to the sixth century BC. It is mentioned in the *Shiji* (an ancient Chinese text), as well as becoming the subject of an instruction book during the Han dynasty. This game – over 2,000 years old – was linked to the Chinese Zodiac, with the pitch representing the earth, the ball a heavenly body, and the various players different Zodiac signs.[6]

Our basic point is therefore made: both past and present, people across the world have played sport. Sport, we might say, is a cultural universal. This is our first proposition.[7]

III

A second proposition: *religion is also a universal.*

Just like sport, religion is woven into the fabric of human life.[8] People invariably understand themselves in relation to the divine.[9] Of course – just like sport – there are regional dialects. Some people speak of faraway gods looking down from on high. Others speak of local gods inhabiting crops and herds. Others will worship the sun, moon and stars. There seems to be no limit to the religious imagination. The stories of the gods are kaleidoscopic.

Though limits are few, family resemblances exist. Whatever theological story is told, the narrative will shape how the people live. It is an understanding of the divine that helps humans make sense of the world. By it we describe the nature of reality and interpret events, but we also determine our rights from our wrongs, with the entire complexity of the moral universe being formed in the telling of the story. What we say about the gods – both positively and negatively – provides the co-ordinates by which a course is plotted through life. Simply put, religion underwrites the meaning humans find in the world.

Religion – to speak again in the most general of terms – is the organized form of behaviour that enables a people to tell their story of the gods. Once holy places are mapped, sacred times set and a hierarchy structured, the theological story will be remembered through ceremonial rituals through which the people attempt to influence – perhaps by way of sacrifice, perhaps by way of prayer – the very gods of which their rituals tell. Why? Because divine blessing is literally vital. Life is in the hands of the gods. Fertility for one, longevity for another, an unhappy god can strike a womb barren, empty the fishermen's nets, fail the farmers' crops and strengthen the tribe's enemy. Humans therefore seek the favour of the gods in order to survive and flourish. The logic of religion is rarely complex. It is *for* life.

As a cultural universal, religion continues to be celebrated across the world. Billions of people navigate their way through life on the basis of the co-ordinates set by their understanding of the gods. Even in the West – despite our best efforts to cultivate atheism – people are unable to shake themselves free of religion. Religion, just like sport, is celebrated everywhere. It remains a cultural universal.

IV

A third proposition (in which we note the relation between our first two points): *historically, sport and religion are intertwined.*

This may come as news to people. The distinction between primordial sports and religion – if it exists at all – is at best fuzzy. Take for example the ancient *Go-jii-ya* race.[10] This annual race bankrolled – and continues to bankroll – the life of the Jicarilla Apaches, an ancient tribe from what is now Texas. The *Go-jii-ya* race is the means by which the Jicarillas guarantee their food by establishing an ordered balance in the provision of nature. According to their theology, the sun and the moon were once in competition. The sun – somewhat confidently – challenged the moon to a race, staking every animal on victory; the moon bet all its fruits. Over the next four years, the sun and the moon won alternate races. This created a pendulum of harvests in the Jicarilla lands, with an abundance of meat one year and too much fruit the next. The people were imperilled by these violent fluctuations, and so the sun and the moon decided to hand the supernatural sport over to the Jicarillas to establish a balance. The regular supply of food depended on the tribe's annual running of the race.

The story of the sun and moon – still handed down faithfully to each generation – underwrites the Jicarillas' *Go-jii-ya* race. The adolescent males – every adolescent has to run at least once before marrying – race along two tracks, the solar and lunar. These two tracks are carefully prepared. Small holes are dug round the circumference and pollen and saplings planted into them. After two days of festival, a fire is ignited and the young runners are decorated with paint, feathers and pollen before being led out into their respective circles by two adolescent girls carrying eagle feathers and corn (symbolizing animals and vegetables). On a given signal, the race begins, with each participant running as fast as they can, though it is not important who wins. For the Jicarillas, only one thing matters: the ceremonial race must be run to sustain their life. Here, the universals of sport and religion intertwine.

A further example underlines the point. For thousands of years, an ancient ball game was played in Central America.[11] In the Aztec language of Náhuatl it was known as *Tlatchtli*. In general, *Tlatchtli* involved a minimum of two players on each side, who would use their hips to move a solid rubber ball (weighing as much as 4 kg) around a high-walled court. The aim of the game was simple. The players had to bounce the rubber ball through a suspended hoop. Simple to play, it was a deeply religious event, heavy with ritual and surrounded by legend. The story again centred on the preservation of the world. Two men played the game at the gates of the underworld. Angered by their noise, the gods had ruthlessly killed the men and hung their severed heads from a tree. One of the severed heads – Hun Hunahpu's – then spat at a passing virgin who fell pregnant. She gave birth to twins who proceeded to challenge the gods to a revenge game. The twins won. The severed heads of their forebears were taken as their prize, with these gruesome trophies becoming the sun and the moon, which then sustained life on Earth. The game of *Tlatchtli* was played to honour this primordial contest. Thereby, it kept the world going.

The game of *Tlatchtli* is depicted in a great deal of surviving artwork from the period. These relics suggest that the gods favoured the victors, though their blessing was not without cost. The losing team is thought to have been sacrificed, their heads cut off, their hearts removed, and their blood poured out for the gods. Some historians even suspect that severed heads were used as the ball.[12] However grizzly the details, it is clear that the game was played amid pictures of human sacrifice as well as ornate sculptures and vases that depicted fruits springing out of severed heads. The fruits show that the game – a cult honouring the community's origin – guaranteed the fertility of the environment. As with the Jicarillas' *Go-jii-ya* race, the game was a ceremonial ritual to preserve life. Sport and religion were again intertwined.

V

These brief historical sketches – cursory though they are – do indicate how difficult it is to distinguish an ancient sport from a religious ritual. Evidence suggests that sport was an important way for ancient people to tell their story of the world *and* a way for them to gain the favour of the gods. Decent harvests, helpful weather, healthy fertility and even the tribes' security were underwritten by elaborate sports-as-ritual.[13] But we must not make too much of this. For a start, it would be a mistake to think that the ancient games are a pure form of sport that reveals its true nature. As we shall see later, the corrupted nature of the fallen world means we cannot read the nature of anything straightforwardly out of human experience. Therefore, *that* ancient sports were religious does not mean that sport itself is. In fact, as we shall see, the truth is much stranger than that.

Notes

1 'Sports are a human universal, appearing in every culture, past and present.' Allen Guttmann, *Sports: The First Five Millennia*, Amherst and Boston: University of Massachusetts Press, 2004, p. 1.

2 The name lacrosse was in fact dreamt up by French colonists. They thought that the stick used in the indigenous game looked a bit like a bishop's crosier. See Stewart Culin, *Games of the North American Indians*, New York: Dover Publications, 1975, p. 399. Forms of the indigenous game are still played; see Tom Rock, 'More than a Game', *Lacrosse Magazine* (November/December 2002).

3 For a helpful account of sport in Africa, see Steve Craig, *Sports and Games of the Ancients*, Westport, CT: Greenwood Press, 2002, pp. 1–38.

4 Guttmann, *Sports*, pp. 9–11.

5 See Rahul Sapra, 'Sports in India', in Dale Hoiberg and Indu Ramchandani (eds), *Students' Britannica India: Select Essays*, New Delhi: Britannica, 2000, pp. 105–10.

6 In a short poem by Li Yu (50–136), for example, we find this: 'A round ball and a square wall, Just like the Yin and the Yang. Moon-shaped goals are opposite each other, Each side has six in number.' Guttmann, *Sports*, p. 40.

7 Simon Barnes, in a wonderfully easy read, estimates that 'sport is about 65 million years old'. Barnes is a great guide through the meaning of sport, though his project ultimately fails. He seems to think he has found meaning in what he sees as a meaningless universe. Simon Barnes, *The Meaning of Sport*, London: Short Books, 2006, pp. 20–1. Another easy read, in which the meaning of sport is nicely explored, is Ed Smith, *What Sport Tells Us about Life*, London: Penguin, 2009.

8 I am indebted to the work of William Baker here. See his *Playing with God*, Harvard University Press, 2007, pp. 1–22.

9 Even if negatively, as with atheism.

10 See Morris Edward Opler, 'The Jicarilla Apache Ceremonial Relay Race', *American Anthropologist* 46.1 (1944), pp. 75–97; Erna Fergusson, *Dancing Gods: Indian Ceremonials of New Mexico and Arizona*, New York: Alfred A. Knopf, 1931, pp. 269–77; Gary Laderman and Luis D. León, *Religion and American Cultures: An Encyclopaedia of Traditions*, vol. 1, Santa Barbara, CA: ABC-CLIO Reference Publishers, 2003, pp. 550–1.

11 See Baker, *Playing with God*, pp. 6–7.

12 Baker, *Playing with God*, p. 7.

13 The connection between sport and blessing is something we still get a sense of in the current obsession over the relation between health and sport. There are few people more (falsely) religious than the fitness fanatic, though – as we shall see – they tend to worship themselves, not God.

2

Classical Sports and Religion

The ritual interweaving of religion and sport is again evident in classical Greek culture. The epic poet Homer – writing around the eighth century BC, though admittedly in mythic form – offers a beautiful description of early Greek sport. In Book XXIII of the *Iliad*, Homer describes the funeral games (*Il.* 23.257–897).[1] These one-off games honoured Patroclos, a friend of Achilles who was killed while fighting the Trojans. Homer tells how Achilles commanded his soldiers to compete for a range of prizes. With betting, advice and quarrels breaking out in the crowd, the games begin with a series of chariot races where the horses and riders pound through the dust. There are then boxing contests, with dynamic pugilists moving like 'leaping fish in weed-strewn shallows', followed by wrestling, sword fights, throwing and footraces. Homer's writing reveals both the variety of sports and the excitement they generated in Greece over 3,000 years ago. Admittedly, there is no explicit calling on the gods in Homer's account. But he does show that the earliest sports functioned as a rite of passage through which Achilles and his men ensured Patroclos' honour in the sight of the gods. There may be no explicit prayers, but the event takes place in the sacred borderlands of life. These are definitely *funeral* games. They take place in the province of the gods.[2]

The connection between Greek sport and religious ritual soon becomes clear, however, with the start of the Olympics. It is not known exactly when the games started, though the eighth century BC seems most likely. We do know the Games quickly grew into a huge spectacle, with athletes and spectators travelling from all over Greece to take part in the event. The third stadium at Olympia – built around 350 BC – held over 40,000 spectators, and the neighbouring hippodrome, where the chariots races took place, had a capacity of around 100,000.[3] Why it was Olympia and not somewhere else that became the site of the Olympics is somewhat mysterious, though it is clear that the place was deeply associated with Zeus, the Father of the gods. There was an ancient altar to him there, which meant that if someone wanted to know how things stood between them and the gods, Olympia was the place to find out. This fact must have featured in the organizers' thinking.[4]

The original programme of sport was limited, with only a single race – won by Koroibos of Elis[5] – run in the first year. The athletics programme, however, was soon expanded to include the *diaulos* ('end and back') and the *dolichos* ('long race'). Over subsequent years, the Games grew larger and larger, soon incorporating the pentathlon, wrestling, boxing and various chariot races. But the growing number of sports never eclipsed the religious character of the Games. Though the event lasted just under a week, the sporting contests only took place on one day, with the rest of the time being given over to more obvious religious activity. The first day was taken up with opening ceremonies, the third day with sacrifices and the fourth day set aside for Zeus. The final day of the meeting was marked with a fantastic feast for the gods.[6]

The religious atmosphere of the Games is difficult for us to imagine. It is clear that they were a model of polytheism, with an altar to the earth goddess Gaea and with funeral rites to gods such as Pelops. That being said, it was Zeus who dominated the event, with his vast temple being the focus of the spectacle. His shrine lay at the foot of a small tree-covered hill, into which a black ram and 100 oxen would be brought and slaughtered.[7] The awful noise of their anguish must have swept through the crowd, just as their blood washed over their feet and stained the walkways. The mountain of ash from these burned carcasses mingled and settled with the bones and offal, creating – we are told – a huge altar of stinking debris, the wreckage of sacrificed life. Olympia was never sanitized. It was (literally) built on sacrifice. Think abattoir.

Into this atmosphere, the athletes would step. Naked as the day they were born, their bodies shimmering with sweat and covered in oil – as the poet Pindar is at pains to tell us – the athletes would suffer greatly under the gruelling summer sun, with extraordinary levels of endurance demanded, their strength and guile tested.[8] Wrestling, for example, involved open-ended grappling contests, with no time limit being set, the match ending only when an opponent was thrown for a third time. Surrounded by cheering crowds, contestants were bathed in oil and covered in dust, their prime physique uncensored and on display to all. The cult of celebrity soon took hold. The athletes became heroes, with victory bringing great honour to the contestant and their home town alike. But true honour was reserved for the gods. The victors would make their way to the temple of Zeus in a long procession – a riotous *kōmos* – beneath a shower of flowers and fruit, a journey that climaxed in the singing of a hymn to Zeus as they received their laurel crown, an event again soaked in sacrifice, with Zeus receiving parcels of bone, fat and offal from the victors.[9] Pindar's songs – such as his Eighth Olympian Ode – celebrate the sacred nature of victory and the way Zeus' blessing is both evidenced *and* realized through it.[10] No question about it, the ancient Olympics were deeply sacred in character.

Though the religious significance of the early Olympics is evident, things are less clear when Greek *gymnasia* began to appear around the fourth century BC. The gymnasium was a place where the male citizens of Greece could escape the noisy bustle of their slave-driven society to wrestle, box and run.[11] As with the Olympics, the young athletes would compete at leisure in the nude – the word *gymnos* literally means unclad (translating *gymnasion* as *nuditorium*)[12] – and soon the public practice of sport was linked to erotic desire. The adolescent athletes became the lovers (*erōmenoi*) of the older citizens as the gymnasia – somewhat strangely if they were meant to prepare men for battle – quickly became centres for leisurely recreation where the physical form could be contemplated as much from the sidelines as pursued through practice.

The gentle leisurely nature of the gym drew the attention of the philosophers. Great minds, such as Socrates, Plato and Aristotle, needed to find space away from the noisy distractions of everyday society to think. The gymnasia became the obvious place to go to.[13] We know that both Plato and Aristotle founded their academies in gyms, and Socrates wandered from gymnasium to gymnasium in search of debate.[14] According to Xenophon, Socrates even rebuked one unfit youth for self-neglect because he was not keeping his body in shape, perhaps recognizing that the unfit life – like the unexamined one – is not worth living.[15] Of course, on first reading, this might appear to contradict our claim that religion and sport are intertwined. We are now talking about philosophers, not priests. Was it not these very philosophers who helped defeat the unsophisticated ruminations of the ancient poets? Did they not expel ornamental myth from the Greek mind and instead pursue rational truth with rigour? If the philosophers wanted to discover the non-sacred nature of *Being* in a gymnasium, surely this proves Greek sport was not wrapped up in religion? Our proposition must be false.

This way of looking at things is a popular reading of the early philosophers. But it is a mistaken reading. There was nothing natural – or universal – about the knowledge being pursued by the likes of Plato or Aristotle. *Being* was simply the name that they chose to give to what is called 'god' in other religious quests.[16] This becomes obvious when we recognize that eternity is the name given by a people to the way in which the passing of time is overcome. Of course, time can be overcome in many ways, one of which is through the gracious or earned protection of any number of gods. But it can also be overcome through the unmoving attributes of *Being*, and, if the *Being* of philosophy is unmasked as the Eternal One in different guise, then life in the gymnasium looks very different: the philosophers' pursuit of beauty, truth and goodness was undertaken amid the physical posturing of the sporting body. Here again, religion and sport were woven together. It is difficult to distinguish the two.[17]

II

As with the Greeks, the Roman culture within which the Church was to find its feet also mixed sport with religion. At its height, the Roman Empire extended from the north of England to the north of Africa, covering over 2 million square miles and incorporating up to 120 million people within its borders. Lasting well over 1,000 years, the empire was made up of hundreds of distinct ethnic, political and economic groupings, a dynamic and shifting amalgamation of ancient traditions and behavioural codes as well as various forms of government. Roman life is therefore difficult to summarize. Nonetheless, the Romans did manage to develop an astonishingly uniform way of life within their vast territories. Both religion and sport featured strongly within it.

The Romans were a deeply religious people. This is evident in the number of gods they worshipped. We now know of hundreds of gods – some major, others minor – who covered just about every contingency under the sun. Each Roman family had their own domestic shrines to their own private spirits (the *Lares Familiares*), which created a further layer of religious practice. And – as the Empire expanded in every direction to encircle the Mediterranean – the number of gods grew ever larger, because Rome wove foreign deities (such as Cybele and Mithra) into the dense indigenous multitude.

The Roman approach to foreign deities was underwritten by their pragmatic belief that their brutal imperial rule would be easier to swallow if a conquered people were allowed to worship their own gods. Yet, whatever the motivation, it meant that Roman citizens were free to worship their own gods while also choosing from an exotic range of foreign deities, becoming religiously bilingual, as one scholar puts it.[18] The vast Pantheon in the centre of Rome – dedicated to 'all gods' – neatly symbolized their approach. Rome was an empire crowded with gods.

The pragmatic approach to deity automatically fuelled an explosion in ritual and festival. Sacrifice, libations and votive offerings happened everywhere and often, with temples – both ancient and novel – springing up across the cityscape. Yet the supply of gods never outstripped demand. This is because the military success of Rome was thought to be insured by the 'Peace of the Gods' – the *Pax deorum* – and this fragile entente meant that the gods' favour needed careful negotiation if the Empire was to flourish. For a good Roman citizen, religion became a duty.[19]

The inflationary economy of Roman religion and imperial success meant that – at its peak under Claudius in the first century – the Roman calendar included 159 days of holiday, marking almost one festival for every day of work.[20] The Romans would mark holidays with large public spectacles, events that were known as the *ludi*. At these events – free to enter and sponsored by the state – huge crowds would gather to watch sports and dramatic performances. Sometimes their ancient myths would be enacted, other times traditional sports such as chariot racing undertaken. Yet, whatever the precise content of the day, it was invariably devoted to the gods. Days included extended ritual and sacrifice to the likes of Ceres or Cybele. Here Roman religion and sport were woven together.

Even when the distinction between the ruler and the gods became blurred (the ruler becoming divine), the religious nature of the events remained unchanged. New festivals (such as the *Ludi Victoriae Sullanae, Ludi Victoriae Caesaris* and *Ludi Fortunae Reducis*) had been introduced to celebrate the military successes of the latest triumphant ruler. But these games essentially elevated the ruler into the realm of the gods rather than secularizing the spectacle itself. By the time of Octavian – the divinely favoured Augustus – the political ruler could be transformed into a god and celebrated in the same way as the gods with only a little mocking from Rome's cultural elite. For the masses, however, there was no escaping it. The *ludi* were religious events.

Within these events, sport assumed an iconic place. It became the primary means by which Rome renegotiated divine favour. Blessing could be sought by means of a fishing contest – in which the eventual winner would sacrifice the winning fish on the sacred Vulcanal rock – or instead by horse races where the winning horse would be decapitated and its blood offered up to the High Priest and Vestal Virgins for cultic use.[21] Even with something as familiar as chariot racing in the Circus Maximus, participants would speed round two posts – the first of which arose from the subterranean altar of Consus – which were themselves linked by an embankment of statues to a range of deities, including Pollentia, the goddess of Might.[22] Whichever way you look at it, sporting events in Rome were soaked in religious significance. They carried 'a heavy religious charge'.[23]

That being said, the matter was more complex than this sketch suggests. Sporting life in Rome was also shaped by a shadowy fusion of long-held traditions and behavioural codes, all of which combined to inform the citizen's self-conscious identity *as* Roman. The concept of *virtus* – embedded deep in Rome's mythology – lay at the heart of the process of self-identification. It loosely translates as 'manliness', the synthetic pinnacle of a number of subsidiary virtues, which include courage, prudence, justice and self-control. *Virtus* was primarily displayed on the battlefield, a place where Roman soldiers could exhibit their excellence in character through noble engagement in hand-to-hand fighting. Being linked to military excellence in this way, the public display of *virtus* soon became an essential feature in any man's bid to run the Empire. It not only enabled entrance into public office (by demonstrating suitable Roman-ness, as it were) but also justified the office-holder's exercise of power once he was in. The ruling elite – in its various oligarchic forms – therefore needed to find ways to display their 'manliness' before the people to legitimize their privileged share in power with the gods. Public spectacles – privately sponsored – became the way to do it.

These spectacular *ludi* began to mark the honour, dignity, reputation and fame of Rome's nobility, a public function that naturally fuelled an inflationary economy of pomp, ceremony and lavish theatrics as rival dynasties sought to outdo each other in the public display of *virtus*.[24] With this rationale driving them, public festivals became increasingly common.[25]

The *munera* – in distinction at first from the public *ludi* – were the natural outcome of this process. These were the gladiatorial contests, which became the most popular symbol of Roman power. The precise genesis of these contests remains largely unknown, though they are thought to have emerged around the third century BC when six gladiators fought in honour of Marcus and Decius Brutus' dead father. Originating as some sort of human sacrifice, the *munera* – a word implying favour or gift – were the way in which the anger of the gods was lessened through the public honouring of their life through the gift of another. As the poet Ausonius believed, the 'blood poured on the ground calmed the scythe-bearing god in the heavens'.[26]

Funded initially by the family of the deceased, the gladiatorial contests soon entered the public domain and – alongside the *ludi* – became hugely popular. Some of these events lasted for days on end, with a crowd of up to 50,000 watching in the purpose-built Colosseum. The gladiators – sometimes up to 11,000 competing in a single festival – would be expertly trained and highly specialized. Some would fight with sword and shield, others with trident and net, while others still would fight against wild animals and beasts. Once thrust into the arena, however, all these differences were transcended. Every gladiator faced death, with the vanquished left to the mercy of the Emperor's extended thumb, which was itself in tune with the popular vote of a vociferous crowd.

These gladiatorial contests were extremely violent and deeply cruel. They were unimaginably brutal spectacles in which thousands of people – and animals – were savagely killed as entertainment. This makes it almost impossible for us to imagine how they made complete sense to the Romans. It is therefore tempting for us to create some sort of myth about the sadistic blood-thirst of an uncivilized and barbaric people. But this move would be a mistake. The Romans had their own reasons for the *munera*. They were the way in which Rome faced reality. They were not senseless violence. They were deeply sacred events.

But how might this be? The *munera* lasted all day. In the morning session – known as the *venationes* – the citizens encountered the brutal reality of nature. Captured beasts – including bears, lions and leopards, not to mention crocodiles, hippos, giraffes and elephants – would be paraded, hunted and killed. In a single hunt, during Pompey's second consulship in 55 BC, spectators watched the slaughter of over 1,000 lions and leopards, as well as seeing a rhinoceros for the first time. This spectacle allowed your average citizen to grasp just how exotic were the lands into which the Empire had spread, as well as seeing how powerful it was in subjugating the beasts. Thus the citizen's initial fear of nature – confronted with a rhinoceros! – was soon cured by the violent defeat of the beasts by the imperial might of Rome. Here the crowd could see, and revel in, the Empire's power over nature.[27]

With the morning's *venationes* complete, the period over lunch was taken up with public executions. Undeniably cruel in form, these events involved dramatic rituals in which the convicted criminal would act out ancient mythological stories about warring gods, but with the criminal being burned to death or brutally castrated in line with the story. Such executions made sense to the Roman mind, especially when the criminal was condemned to the beasts (*damnatio ad bestias*). If someone chose to step outside the civilizing norm of Roman law – to enter the state of nature, as it were – then they were effectively casting themself out of civilization and into nature. What better way to face the consequence of your decision than by meeting nature in tooth and claw? It made sense to throw criminals to the lions.[28]

With the executions complete, the crowd's attention would turn to the gladiatorial contests. Here the citizen – the citizen of a society where three out of five people died in their twenties – could learn how to die *well*.[29] Death was to be accepted without protest, the defeated gladiator puffing out his chest, leaning to the right, head lowered, half-seated on his weapons as he was dispatched with honour.[30] Of course, the gory nature of the killing would have appealed to the sadistic among the crowd. But the majority of people were more interested in the *dying* than the killing. Here they could witness true 'manliness', the cardinal virtue of *virtus* again. This is why loud boos would ring out if the final drama was ill performed. It is also why the fallen gladiator – if able to face death honourably – would often be rewarded by the crowd's loud cheers, cheers that would then leverage the Emperor's thumb upwards and secure the freedom of the vanquished. The *munera* were socially complex events.

But in what way were these events religious? On the surface, they were political, to do with the social ordering of Roman society. They were a 'fortifying lesson in the triumph of civilization'.[31] Though religious symbols were everywhere – with Dis Pater commissioned to drag off the dead, Mercury finishing off any possible pretenders and Pluto accompanying bodies out of the amphitheatre beneath colourful images of Nemesis in a dramatized ritual of journeying to the underworld[32] – the events primarily conveyed the story of Rome, not the gods.[33] With the parade and slaughter of animals, the spectators were celebrating the lofty dominion of Roman man; with the public executions – attended by vergers dressed as Mercury and Charon – they witnessed the struggle between law and chaos; and, with the gladiators, the crowd revelled in the triumph of Roman power over death, with *virtus* ensuring the clemency of the crowd, and the Emperor – the personification of Rome itself – holding the power of life and death in his hands.[34] But this was precisely the point at which politics merged with religion. The Emperor – now divinized – was celebrated as the judge of the living and the dead.[35] Roman politics had become the sporting spectacle of self-worship; it was all about the eternal nature of Rome. This was a problem for the early Church. Here was an idolatrous imposter. The Emperor was not the true Judge of the living and the dead. Jesus Christ is that man.

Notes

1 See Matthew W. Dickie, 'Fair and Foul Play in the Funeral Games in the Iliad', *Journal of Sport History* 11.2 (1984), pp. 8–17.

2 Homer also writes of sports in Book VIII of the *Odyssey*. In this book, Odysseus is washed ashore among the Phaeacians. The Phaeacians have a contest,

with running, fighting and various throwing events (such as discus). They quickly challenge Odysseus, who is enticed into action through insult and dare. Yet Odysseus knows what the contest is really about: this has to do with the gods. He picks up the biggest discus and hurls it much further than any of theirs, and is therefore seen as a god in human form. See discussion in Nigel Spivey, *The Ancient Olympics*, 2nd edn, Oxford: Oxford University Press, 2012, pp. 6–7.

3 Allen Guttmann, *Sports: The First Five Millennia*, Amherst and Boston, MA: University of Massachusetts Press, 2004, p. 19.

4 Spivey, *Ancient Olympics*, pp. 179–82.

5 Koroibos was either a cook or the performer of ritual sacrifice. If it was the latter job, it fits nicely with our thesis here.

6 It is also of note that the Games were announced in each region by a *theoros*, a personal ambassador for the gods who invited people to come and engage in religion. David Potter, *The Victor's Crown: A History of Ancient Sport from Homer to Byzantium*, London: Quercus, 2011, p. 57.

7 See description in Spivey, *Ancient Olympics*, pp. xxi–xxv.

8 Spivey, *Ancient Olympics*, pp. 142–3.

9 Spivey, *Ancient Olympics*, pp. 134–6.

10 Spivey, *Ancient Olympics*, pp. 143–5.

11 See Guttmann, *Sports*, p. 18.

12 Spivey, *Ancient Olympics*, p. 34.

13 The link between the early philosophical academies and the sporting gymnasia has been well documented, with even the English word *school* being rooted in the Greek word for *leisure*. See Josef Pieper, *Leisure: The Basis of Culture*, trans. Gerald Malsbary, South Bend, IN: St Augustine's Press, 1998.

14 See Spivey, *Ancient Olympics*, pp. 44–53.

15 Xenaphon in the *Memorabilia*, Book III.12.

16 This point draws from the work of Robert Jenson, who offers an expert account on the theological character of philosophy. Robert W. Jenson, *Systematic Theology*, vol. 1, *The Triune God*, New York and Oxford: Oxford University Press, 1997, pp. 3–22.

17 Once it is (mistakenly) decoupled from religion, the gymnasium is often imagined to be a place where the citizens prepare for war. But the Greeks' passion for sport cannot be reduced to military exercise, even if it is a side effect to sport. Alexander the Great recognized the problem here when he asked – in the overrun city of Miletus, with its many statues of successful athletes – 'where were the men with such bodies when the barbarians laid siege to your city?' Further, if sport served war, why would the citizens of Athens spend five days – and 100,000 drachma – honouring the god Dionysos when it would surely be more productive to spend the money on weapons or regimented drills? Sport was never fully rationalized as military training. There is not 'some necessary or binding equation', as Spivey shows. Or, to put it another way, of course sport will serve war if your gods are warring. Spivey, *Ancient Olympics*, pp. 25–8. We will explore the relation between sport and war in Chapter 9.

18 Christopher Kelly, *The Roman Empire: A Very Short Introduction*, Oxford: Oxford University Press, 2006, p. 28.

19 See Jerome Carcopino, *Daily Life in Ancient Rome: The People and the City at the Height of the Empire*, Kindle edn, 2008, pp. 121–30.

20 Carcopino, *Daily Life in Ancient Rome*, pp. 205–6.

21 Carcopino, *Daily Life in Ancient Rome*, p. 206.

22 Carcopino, *Daily Life in Ancient Rome*, p. 213.

23 Peter Brown, *Through the Eye of a Needle: Wealth, the Fall of Rome and the Making of Christianity in the West, 350–550 AD*, Princeton, NJ: Princeton University Press, 2012, p. 103.

24 See Eckart Köhne, 'Bread and Circuses: The Politics of Entertainment', in Eckart Köhne, Cornelia Ewigleben and Ralph Jackson (eds), *Gladiators and Caesars: The Power of the Spectacle in Ancient Rome*, Berkeley and Los Angeles, CA: University of California Press, 2000, pp. 8–30. For the way the Games were used for the personal display of wealth, see Brown, *Through the Eye of a Needle*, pp. 66–8. Brown argues that the rich tried to outdo each other in what became 'a sort of financial sumo wrestling' (p. 86).

25 'Going to the games was one of the practices which went with being a Roman.' Kelly, *Roman Empire*, p. 79.

26 Cited in Carcopino, *Daily Life in Ancient Rome*, p. 207.

27 Thomas Wiedemann, *Emperors and Gladiators*, London and New York: Routledge, 1992, pp. 3, 65. See also Brown, *Through the Eye of a Needle*, pp. 116–7.

28 Wiedemann, *Emperors and Gladiators*, pp. 85–88.

29 Wiedemann, *Emperors and Gladiators*, p. 93.

30 'Gladiators were trained not only to fight well, but also to die properly, chest out, leaning to the right, head drooping, half-seated on their weapons . . . a cool, formalized way of death, which, if not properly performed, would be loudly booed by a disapproving crowd.' Kelly, *Roman Empire*, p. 81.

31 Brown, *Through the Eye of a Needle*, p. 117.

32 Note: 'fatal encounter in the amphitheatre was predictably ritualized in terms of the transition to the underworld: "Larvae" . . . hounded cowardly recruits, "Mercury" prodded corpses with a brand to test their lifelessness, and "Pluto" accompanied the bodies out the arena.' K. M. Coleman, 'Fatal Charades: Roman Executions Staged as Mythological Enactments', *Journal of Roman Studies* 80 (1990), p. 67, see pp. 44–73 for general point.

33 In Chapter 1, we offered a working definition of religion, which is worth keeping in mind here. Religion – to speak in the most general of terms – is the organized form of behaviour that enables a people to tell their story of the gods through ceremonial rituals through which the people attempt to influence the very gods of which their rituals tell. For the Romans, the story of the rulers was merged with the story of the gods. Politics and religion became one in a way that is hard for us to imagine today.

34 Wiedemann, *Emperors and Gladiators*, pp. 85–8.

35 By the beginning of the Common Era, the possession of *virtus* had assumed a quasi-divine character within public life, with the neatest of equations presenting itself to the vainest of the emperors: the virtuous Ruler was himself the personification of deity.

3

The Early Church's View of Sport

The early Church had a great deal to think about. The unimaginable events of Easter and Pentecost had forced the disciples to rethink the very nature of Israel's God, as well as their own identity within his ongoing action. Fuelled by Jesus' call to spread the good news – and scattered far and wide by persecution – Christianity spread rapidly across the Roman Empire. Right from the start, the implications of the gospel were being worked out in time, in culture.

Christian identity is a simple-yet-complex matter, with the gospel's relation to the ongoing life of Israel and the patterns of Gentile life endlessly negotiable. Nothing dropped from the sky and little was set in stone, though someone had been raised from the dead. Quite quickly, a process of initial welcome and full participation within the community's life did fall into place, with the internal orderings of the Church's sacramental life operating as a boundary by which to distinguish the Church from the cultures in which it was embedded. The early Christians were quickly identified as a set-apart community, clearly distinct from the norm. They *lived* differently.

With authoritative texts such as Paul's letters and the four Gospels soon complementing Israel's Scriptures – and rules for right reading circulating alongside them – the early Christians were able to work out in ever greater detail what a gospel-shaped life might look like. Questions surrounding marriage and dietary habits were immediately addressed, as well as the Church's internal ordering of liturgical action and its response to Jewish practices such as circumcision. With the Spirit's unfailing help, the good news of Jesus of Nazareth was becoming increasingly universal, not just in geographic scope but in ontological depth.[1] *Everything* was to be informed in thanksgiving to Jesus.

With the question of Christian identity being asked, the early Church needed to work out how to handle the sporting spectacles of their day. Could Christians participate in these spectacles – as sponsors, spectators or competitors – or would they be better advised to steer clear of events? These questions could not be ducked. Sporting events were far too popular to remain unaddressed. The public games were extremely well attended. The Greek pursuit of bodily excellence had merged with lavish Roman spectacle to produce truly amazing events in which athletes, charioteers and gladiators competed in a variety of dramatic contests. In the eastern part of the Empire – in which Christianity had spread rapidly – any decent-sized city would host an event, with the Isthmian games at Corinth being a good example. Here thousands of citizens – both local and visiting – gathered together to cheer on the athletes as they competed in boxing matches, wrestling tournaments and high-speed chariot races, with the competitors struggling to attain the famed pine wreath. But it was by no means obvious what a Christian should make of these events. Could sport play a part in a life oriented to Christ?[2]

The Church's Scriptures – initially, of course, only the Old Testament – were of little immediate help, offering no explicit directive for the early Christians to follow.[3] Christians could turn to the creation story, where they discover a positive view of embodied life, with human physicality being celebrated in the catch-all pronouncement that everything is 'very good' (Gen. 1.31) – though the third chapter of Genesis quickly muddies the waters. The Deuterocanonical books, however – questionable authorities for some Christians today, but widely accepted as authoritative in the early Church – *do* mention sport directly, though admittedly only in passing. These books tell of a gymnasium being built in Jerusalem during the latter part of the second century BC, although reference to this project is quite negative in character, being set within the story of Israel's idolatrous acceptance of rival customs (1 Mac. 1.14 and 2 Mac. 4.9). At best, the Deuterocanonical books underlined the questionable nature of sport. However, they do not judge whether sport is good or bad in itself.

The writings of St Paul looked a more promising resource. Sport was clearly on Paul's mind as he wrote. He regularly uses illustrations from the sporting world, referencing sports such as running, boxing, chariot racing and even – arguably – gladiatorial contests.[4] Paul was certainly prepared to harness sport's grip on the imagination, and was clearly familiar with the popular sports of his day. He may even have attended various games in various cities during his travels. Whether he believed sport was a good thing or not, however, is a lot less obvious.

Nonetheless, Paul's use of sporting images has encouraged many Christians over the centuries to draw a straight line between his thinking and a positive view of sport. Recently, Pope John Paul II – to take an illustrious example – did exactly this, employing 1 Corinthians 9.24 as grounds for celebrating sport ('Do you not know that in a race all the runners compete, but only one receives the prize? Run in such a way that you may win it').[5] However, in a text such as this, Paul is only *using* a sporting image to make a wider point about discipleship. He appreciates that athletes approach life with one eye on a race. What they eat, how they rest, even their sex life, is subsumed into their training regime. Everything serves optimal performance. Paul's point, therefore, is not that running is good, but that the gospel demands something similar of the disciple. Christians must fix their eyes on the prize ahead, allowing it to shape their entire lives.

The eternal nature of the prize on offer means – if anything – that Paul's rhetoric casts sport in a negative light. When compared to the Christian life, the life of an athlete is empty, a mere punching of the air, an aimless run, a fading garland that withers away. If we wanted to draw a straight line from Paul's rhetoric to a theology of sport, this negative contrast would be as far as we would get. This is not to deny that Paul's underlying theology of the body could inform a positive theology of sport. Paul is opposed to the hedonistic misuse of the body, as well as to its outright denigration. He wants Christians to order their whole life to the glory of God, which includes their bodies. 'Do you not know that your body is a temple . . . therefore glorify God in your body' (1 Cor. 6.19–20). Here Paul's thinking is being shaped by the incarnation. Because God the Son is embodied, the Christian life cannot be opposed to embodiment. Bodies are good because of Jesus. This could be a foundation for an early theology of sport. Nonetheless, we must be clear here. Paul is not discussing sport in his letters. He is therefore neither baptizing it nor condemning it outright. The biblical jury remains out.

II

The early Church therefore needed to think through the question of sport *themselves*. However, the intellectual world in which they studied was deeply dualistic, radically separating spirit from matter. Material embodiment was often seen as the problem that a religion was meant to solve. Being formed in this spirit-loving environment – and all too aware of the reality of the Fall – the early theologians began on the back foot. They can be found warning their congregations about the perilous nature of embodiment. We find Basil the Great – in the fourth century – declaring war on the body's 'chaotic stirrings', arguing that only a hatred of the body can counter the sensual desires that plague the Christian life.[6] Ambrose of Milan – commentating on Luke's Gospel – also disparaged the body, depicting it at best as the soul's clothing, at worst a dungeon from which the soul must escape.[7] Given their deeply ingrained suspicion, these comments make sense. But it means we are unlikely to find a ringing endorsement for sport in the Fathers' work.

Yet, despite their misgivings, the Fathers were not entirely negative. The logical trajectory of divine incarnation and physical resurrection – something Irenaeus spelt out early on in the tradition – meant that pessimism could not have the final word. We therefore find Tertullian recognizing the essential role of the body in salvation, being neither somehow secondary to the soul nor destined for destruction.[8] Cyril of Jerusalem likewise ends up rejoicing in embodiment despite holding some serious doubts about the corrupted nature of our bodies. In his preparations for baptism, he recognizes the fallen desires of the body one moment before marvelling at the 'wonderful body' – with its delicate structure – the next.[9] This twofold pattern – of warning and marvelling – can also be found in the work of John Chrysostom. In his thirteenth homily on Romans, Chrysostom echoes the struggles of St Paul in Romans 7, railing against the flesh in the 'whirl and thraldom of passions' but refusing to equate it with the body, which is a created good.[10] The early Church therefore found itself saying two things at once. Bodies are good. Bodies are dangerous.

Amid this intellectual turbulence, the Fathers had to think through the question of sport. Of course, with Paul as their forerunner, the early theologians were happy to use sporting images in their sermons. In his preaching on virtue, for example, John Chrysostom draws from a wide range of sports to teach the faithful about the good life.[11] Christians are encouraged to look to God as their example just as a wrestler will look to a trainer, and – he adds – if it is stupid for a wrestler to learn from either a greengrocer or fishmonger, then it is doubly foolish for Christians to look anywhere other than God to learn about life.[12] Similarly, Chrysostom uses the trials of the athlete – naked under the hot scorching sun – as a way to encourage his fellow Christians to help each other amid their ongoing struggle.[13] This rhetorical point is sharpened in his thirteenth homily on the Letter to the Philippians where the winning tactic of a runner – head raised, eyes focused on the path, thereby dodging the slippery soil and remaining steady on his or her feet – is used to teach Christians their own need for discipline as they seek their own prize.[14] Just like Paul, Chrysostom is using sporting imagery to serve his argument. But would the early Christians be prepared to use sport in service to their *life*?

The Fathers' approach to bathing gives us an insight here. Bathing was extremely popular at this time, with users of the bathhouses enjoying not just the steam rooms, saunas and warm pools but also the outdoor gymnasium where ball games and athletic disciplines (such as throwing the discus) were the most popular ways to work up a healthy sweat. Clement of Alexandria – writing around the turn of the third century – acknowledged that many of his congregation were attending the baths, and he knew that some of them were attending simply for pleasure. He judges this to be quite wrong – with little explanation – and therefore expressly forbidden. But, as Clement sees it, a trip to the bathhouse *can* improve health, cleanse the skin and generate warmth to the benefit of the Christian. His overall conclusion is simple: 'Unless the bath is for some use, we ought not to indulge in it.'[15]

Other Fathers also offered qualified endorsements of bathing. Tertullian, for example, was happy to visit the baths on a regular basis, though he was careful to avoid them during the Saturnalia – an ancient Roman festival in December – when widespread debauchery made their use unsafe.[16] Likewise Gregory of Nyssa saw bathing as an appropriate comfort for everyday life, though it was not to be misused for pleasure.[17] For the church Fathers, therefore, it seems that bathing was permissible only under certain conditions. None of them fully endorsed it. Just as with sporting imagery, use did not imply validation.[18] But what exactly was their problem?

III

The problem with sport was fairly straightforward. As we have seen, sporting events were inextricably bound up with the religious rituals of the day. Games were riddled with sacred symbol and meaning. Host cities would be filled with travelling fortune-tellers, magicians and pagan priests, and the streets would be lined with food stalls, souvenir sellers and relics as well. Competing athletes and adjudicating officials would be purified through sacrifice and the taking of oaths, with every aspect of their efforts being ordered towards the host deity.[19]

Someone like Tertullian, therefore, quickly recognized that this was a problem for the Christian. In his mind, chaired by priests, crowned with sin and stained by false worship, the sacrificial reality of the Games made them too dangerous.[20] Christians should neither applaud the stupid races nor celebrate the ridiculous athletics, and the athletes' misshaped bodies – disfigured by training and diet – were to be understood as a visible, tangible symbol of a culture's rebellion against God. Tertullian was therefore adamant. Anyone who had made a promise at baptism to reject the works of the devil must not participate in such devil-driven events.[21] As he saw it, Christians should not be the 'Devil's guest'.[22]

With this in mind, Tertullian carefully countered the various arguments that were circulating in favour of sport. Enjoyment cannot be baptized, he contended, as the Church's life – resting on the martyrs – can never be defined by pleasure. Nor can appeal to sport being 'natural' justify Christian participation, because nature is ethically neutral, something evident when we consider how natural materials can be shaped into lethal weapons. And, Tertullian contends, even if God remains undefiled as he gazes disapprovingly on sport, this does not mean that Christians will likewise remain pure. Instead, sport will make them mad, angry and discordant, with all their abusive taunts having no place in the Christian life. Tertullian's final answer was therefore clear: sport is to be avoided.[23]

Tertullian was not alone. John Chrysostom criticizes his local games, again focusing his argument on the idolatrous nature of the events. To Chrysostom's mind, the Games at Daphne were irreparably tainted by their pompous processions in which demons danced and the devil was lauded.[24] He therefore preached against the Games, barring Christians from entering what he deemed an idolatrous temple and from joining in the evil celebrations, grounds on which he rejected both athletics and horseracing.[25] Likewise, Clement of Alexandria's 'instructor' banned people from the spectacles, seeing the racecourse as 'the seat of plagues'.[26] Of course, every rule has its exception. We do find a Phrygian inscription from the third century which suggests a Christian sponsored the local games, and Jerome tells the story of Hilarion who blessed one Christian's horses, stables and racecourse to counter the magical spells of his opponents.[27] But though a couple of exceptions exist, the basic position of the church Fathers was clear. As Novatian put it, 'idolatry is the mother of all games'.[28]

The Fathers' opposition to sport soon found formal expression. In AD 314, the first Council of Arles – in a series of canons covering issues such as the timing of Easter and the rebaptism of apostates – decreed that Christians were not to fraternize with gladiators and charioteers. The penalty for doing so was excommunication.[29] The assembled bishops were only confirming what had been preached from the start, but now it was official. Sport is dangerous for Christians.[30]

IV

The early Church's approach to sport therefore has a twofold character. Sport is to be opposed on the grounds of idolatry, though it can be used on occasion for health or teaching purposes. There is, however, a third feature of the early Church's history that we should not overlook. Alongside use and opposition, we discover the unstoppable popularity of sport.

On one reading, the decision at Arles shows this. Christians must still have been participating in sports at this time. If they were not, there would be little point in saying they cannot. No doubt, sports would have been part of many Christians' past. They would have loved sport before their conversion. Some of them would therefore find it hard to give up once they were baptized. Augustine's friend Alypius seems a case in point (as his friends were able to draw him *back* to the Games against his will, though this was in the early stages of his conversion).[31] But there seems to be more at work here than simply old habits dying hard. This becomes evident once Constantine converts to Christianity in 312. Christianity was now the favoured religion of the Empire, with local deities – initially tolerated –

eventually outlawed along with sacrifices, libations, garlands and divination. Sports were also soon banned, with Constantine prohibiting gladiatorial games in 325. Nevertheless, despite a double imperial–ecclesial ban, the games continued. Some were held in Antioch three years after the ban was introduced, and Constantine's own sons were still giving permission for games as late as 337, over a decade after the edict.[32] Theodosius I did eventually bring about their end in 393[33] – and within 30 years the Temple of Zeus at Olympia was burned down, its statue destroyed, and the heart of the gaming culture exorcised[34] – yet it still took until the fifth century for Emperor Honorius to get the gladiatorial schools to close. Even then some of the *munera* seemed to have lasted a few more decades. What we need note, therefore, is this: though the full weight of the imperial–ecclesial power was behind it, prohibition proved hard to enforce. Sport was deeply popular. It seemed almost irresistible.[35]

This is especially the case with chariot racing. Unlike gladiatorial combat and athletic events, charioteering continued through into the eleventh century.[36] As a sport, it had not been without its critics in the early Church, with the stain of associated pagan ritual a problem for the Fathers. Though Tertullian did recognize that horse riding is natural, he argued that as soon as the horse and chariot are taken into the circus they pass into the service of demons. Likewise, Clement of Alexandria saw the racecourse as the 'seat of plagues'.[37] Nonetheless, chariot racing remained popular. Therefore, Emperor Theodoric in the fifth century – having grown weary with endless prohibition – began to take a more pragmatist approach to it. He recognized the way charioteering had become overly politicized, with teams being aligned to party political factions. As the Emperor saw it, charioteering should therefore be controlled rather than banned. It was to be taken under the dominion of the Emperor as his gift, a sign of his grace.[38] Pagan symbols were to be stripped away and replaced with Christian ones. Proceedings would begin with the sign of the cross, before hymns glorifying God and Mary were sung.[39] The Christianization of these races went so far as teams being aligned to doctrinal positions, with the Blues and the Greens becoming linked to those who argue that God was triune and those who questioned whether Jesus had two natures.[40] The sport was now coated thickly with Christian varnish. As uneasy as it proved, an alliance between Christianity and charioteering had been created. The long-standing realpolitik of 'bread and circuses' had won out.[41] The Emperor had recognized that sport was so popular it could not be stopped. It should therefore be used for political ends.

But what can we make of all this today? First and foremost, history is messy. There is no single approach that leaps from the pages of history. Instead, the Church's approach to sport is multifarious. Nonetheless, we can identify three distinct notes from our survey. These notes combine to form a first sounding from Church history.

First, the early Church *used* sport by setting it to serve its own purpose, be that in rhetorical imagery or conditional acceptance in service to health, self-discipline and even political peace. Sport was acceptable if it was put to *use*.

Second, the Church also pronounced that sport is *unacceptable*. Primarily because of its long association with pagan religion, participation was regarded as an idolatrous denial of baptismal promises. Christians were to be deeply suspicious about sport, handling it – at a minimum – with great care. Idolatry is the mother of all games.

But, third, the history of the early Church suggests that sport is deeply *popular*. Despite being attacked from pulpit and throne, people – Christian and non-Christian alike – continued to flock to events. Something about sport makes it hard to give up. We should take note.

The Church's early history therefore sounds three distinct notes: instrumentalism, opposition and popularity. The question for us is whether these notes fade away or whether they instead resound through the course of history. To answer this question, we will briefly look at two other periods in the Church's history: the medieval Church's approach to sport and that of the Protestant churches. We turn first to the Middle Ages.[42]

Notes

1 Ontology is the study of reality, existence, being and becoming. In this instance, it is to claim that Jesus makes a difference to *everything*. He is Lord.

2 In what follows, I am guided primarily by the work of Alois Koch SJ, 'Biblical and Patristic Foundations for Sport', in Kevin Lixey, Christoph Hübenthal, Dietmar Mieth and Norbert Müller (eds), *Sport and Christianity: A Sign of the Times in the Light of Faith*, Washington: Catholic University of America Press, 2012, pp. 81–103. Readers are advised to make use of this valuable resource. An electronic version is available at Alois Koch SJ, *The Christian View on Sport: Foundations in the Holy Scriptures and in the Church Fathers' Writings*, lecture given in Mainz, 2 March 2007, available at http://www.conspiration.de/koch/english/menschenbild-e.html.

3 A brief aside: Bryan Mason manages to find some humorous references to various sports in the Scriptures. Tennis: 'Joseph served in Pharaoh's court' (Genesis 41). Football: Jesus was left-back in Jerusalem (Luke 2). Cricket (wicketkeeper): 'Elijah made loud appeals to the Lord and knocked over all the baals' (1 Kings 18). Bryan Mason, *The Teaching of Physical Education: A Biblical Perspective*, The Christian Institute, 2002, available at: http://www.christian.org.uk/html-publications/education9.htm. We could also add: 'press on towards the goal' (Phil. 3.14) and Paul and Barnabas being sent off (Acts 13.3).

4 For running, see 2 Timothy 4.7; for boxing, see 1 Corinthians 9.26; for chariot racing, see Philippians 3.13–14; and for gladiators, see Philippians 1.27–30. For a helpful discussion of all the metaphors used by Paul, see Shirl James Hoffman, *Good Game: Christianity and the Culture of Sports*, Waco, TX: Baylor University Press, 2010, pp. 41–5.

5 John Paul II, 'Jubilee Year of the Redeemer: Homily Given at the Olympic Stadium in Rome, 12 April 1984', in Kevin Lixey, Norbert Müller and Cornelius Schafer (eds), *Blessed John Paul II Speaks to Athletes: Homilies, Messages and Speeches on Sport*, London: John Paul II Sports Foundation, 2012, p. 21.

6 Basil the Great, *To Young Men on the Right Use of Greek Literature* VIII.

7 Ambrose of Milan, *On Luke* V.107 and VIII.48; see also Ambrose's funeral oration to his brother (II.40), all available in Koch, 'Biblical and Patristic Foundations for Sport'.

8 See Tertullian, *On the Resurrection of the Flesh*.

9 Cyril of Jerusalem, *Catechetical Lecture* 4.22.

10 John Chrysostom, *13th Homily on Romans*.

11 I here again draw on the work of Koch, 'Biblical and Patristic Foundations for Sport', where full references to (and quotations from) Migne's *Patrolgia Graeca* (henceforth *PG*) can be found.

12 *PG* 58, 665ff, cited in Koch.

13 *PG* 51, 125, cited in Koch.

14 *PG* 62, 271ff, cited in Koch.

15 Clement of Alexandria, *The Instructor* III.9, and see III.10 for his qualified approval of gymnastics and the place of physical exercise in health.

16 Tertullian, *Apology*, see Chapter 42.

17 Gregory Nyssa, *Homily on the Sermon on the Mount* 7.

18 And as with bathing, the Fathers placed certain conditions on participation in other sports. Clement of Alexandria, for example, recognized that gymnastics has many benefits, being good for body and soul in encouraging disciplined self-improvement. So long as it does not distract Christians from more worthy activities, Clement sees little wrong with it. He is also open to wrestling and ball games on the same grounds, though again cautions against excessive vanity in taking part. Clement, *The Instructor* III.10.

19 See Hoffman, *Good Game*, p. 27.

20 Tertullian, *The Shows* XI.

21 Tertullian, *The Shows* XXIII.

22 Tertullian, *The Shows* XXVIII.

23 Tertullian, *The Shows* XX. Tertullian refuses to make a special case out of spectating: 'nowhere and never is that permitted which is not permitted always and everywhere'. The dangers of watching sport are well recorded in Christian literature, for example, Cassiodorus – the secretary to Emperor Theodosius at the end of the fourth century – argued that the popular sporting spectacles undermined society, cultivating immoral citizens who were schooled in dishonesty and fickle partisan allegiances. 'The spectacle drives out sound morality and invites childish factiousness, it banishes honesty and it is an unfailing source of riots . . . most remarkable of all, in these beyond all other spectacles men's minds are carried away by excitement without any regard for dignity and sobriety. [In the races] Green takes the lead and half the crowd is plunged into gloom. Blue passes him, and a great mass of citizens suffer the torments of the damned. They cheer wildly with no useful result; they suffer nothing but are cut to the heart.' Cited in Hoffman, *Good Game*, p. 38.

24 See *PG* 49, 370 and *PG* 50, 645, cited in Koch.

25 *PG* 59, 188, cited in Koch.

26 Clement, *The Instructor* II.11.

27 See Jermone, *The Life of Saint Hilarion* XVI and XX, though Hilarion is clearly not a fan of sport and is again *using* it to witness to the Lordship of Christ.

28 Novatian, *The Spectacle*. The Church's opposition to gladiatorial combat had little to do with pacifism (which will surprise those who equate sport with preparation for war), nor was it based on a notion of human rights (contrary to those who see the cruelty of sport as the problem) – nor animal rights for that matter. See discussion in Allen Guttmann, *Sports: The First Five Millennia*, Amherst and Boston, MA: University of Massachusetts Press, 2004, pp. 32–3.

29 Canon 4 is straightforward. Charioteers are to be excommunicated. Canon 3 is a little more ambiguous. There is reference to 'laying down arms'. This has been interpreted to refer to gladiators, not least because the following canons also refer to actors at the games and the language is similar to that employed by Constantine when banning the games. See Charles Joseph Hefele, *A History of the Christian Councils from the Original Documents*, 2nd edn, 1.3.15, London: T & T Clark, 1883, pp. 185–7.

30 Hoffman shows how the *Apostolic Constitutions* of the fourth century, for example – which were thought to be derived from the apostles and accepted as canonical by John of Damascus – had been formally calling on Christians to avoid 'indecent spectacles', forbidding baptism and communion to those visiting the stadiums and amphitheatres. Hoffman, *Good Game*, p. 37.

31 Augustine, *Confessions* VIII. St Jerome could comment that those who were 'yesterday in the amphitheatre, [were] today in the church; [who] in the evening [were] at the circus [are] in the morning at the altar'. Cited in Hoffman, *Good Game*, p. 36. Though some no doubt fell to temptation, even by the third century a Christian convert like Cyprian could pinpoint his rejection of the games as the key moment in his conversion.

32 Hoffman, *Good Game*, p. 41. Some games, such as the animal hunts (the *venationes*), enjoyed a 100-year stay of execution. See Guttmann, *Sports*, p. 33.

33 *Theodosian Code* 16.10.17, cited in David Potter, *The Victor's Crown: A History of Ancient Sport from Homer to Byzantium*, London: Quercus, 2011, p. 311.

34 Nigel Spivey, *The Ancient Olympics*, 2nd edn, Oxford: Oxford University Press, 2012, pp. 208–10.

35 Peter Brown's magisterial survey of the relationship between the Roman nobility and the early Church is helpful here. Though Brown focuses on the question of wealth – and the way the Church competed with sporting spectacles for the nobility's money – he shows us that the conversion of Constantine did not change everything immediately. Noble families – some even Christian – would put on games that would still cause 'the raw, pre-Christian adrenalin of worship' to run through Roman veins (p. 103). In effect, the lines of history are not as clear as we are making out here, but the general point remains: the Church, through time, did distinguish sport from worship in a way which was previously unimaginable. See Peter Brown, *Through the Eye of a Needle: Wealth, the Fall of Rome and the Making of Christianity in the West, 350–550 AD*, Princeton: Princeton University Press, 2012. Brown also makes the point that the sons of some bishops were condemned for putting on shows after the imperial ban. This shows how messy history can be (p. 75).

36 Hoffman, *Good Game*, p. 48.

37 Tertullian, *The Shows* IX; Clement of Alexandria, *The Instructor* XI.

38 See Hoffman, *Good Game*, p. 48. For the place of political pressure groups in sport, see also Brown, *Through the Eye of a Needle*, p. 66.

39 Peter Brown again makes the case that a lot of the nobility are better understood to be 'crypto pagans' at this time, who looked upon Christianity with disdain, continuing to function effectively as pagans, not least in the putting on of sporting events, which were 'sound-proof to Christianity' (though gladiators disappeared). Brown, *Through the Eye of a Needle*, pp. 458–61. Brown makes the case that most of the Roman nobility 'were unimpressed by the either–or choice presented to them by the clergy' (p. 75).

40 Hoffman, *Good Game*, p. 49.

41 Cf. Juvenal, *Satire* X.77–81.

42 Hoffman also identifies a tripartite approach to sport in the early Church: ambivalence and unease, periodic attempts to ban or control, followed by periods of co-opting, harnessing it for mission. Hoffman, *Good Game*, p. 48.

4

Case Study (I): Sport and the Medieval Catholic Church

History is complex. It is driven by kaleidoscopic and multi-farious forces that interact and interconnect, producing a wide range of patterns that are often discernible only in hindsight – and that is before we bring God into the equation. It is there-fore wrong to attribute significant change to any single factor. Nonetheless, Constantine's conversion did mark the beginning of a new era. A Christian was now in power. This meant that the followers of Jesus Christ were no longer being fed to lions or slaughtered by gladiators. Instead, they were being drawn into the very centre of public life. From this central vantage point, Christians could begin to shape Roman life more fully.[1]

With Christianity's establishment, the gospel increasingly drove social innovation and reform, with Roman society being fashioned over time by explicit Christian values and perspectives. *Christendom* – the reality of a theocratic polity – lay this side of the horizon, with the Church (somewhat ambitiously) attempting to baptize an entire culture. But sport was also quietly changing while all this was going on. Over the coming decades, gladiators and athletes would give way to charioteers, who in turn – over centuries – were to be replaced by the spectacle of tournaments and jousting knights. Nothing stood still. The question for us to consider is whether these changes altered the Church's approach to sport or, instead, did the threefold chord – of use, opposition and popularity – reverberate through history?

II

To many a mind, the sight of a valiant knight, astride his horse amid bright pageantry – armour-plated, visor down and thundering towards a rival – epitomizes the Middle Ages.[2] During this period, tournaments and jousts were held across Europe, though their popularity seems to have centred in the northern regions of France (and have been minimal in the Iberian Peninsula).[3] Knights errant – true to their name – would wander from contest to contest, being met by large crowds and chorused with popular chants as they battled for honour and prestige in this exciting sport.

The sport of tourneying – distinct from an individual joust – developed out of the feudal system, a political economy that seemed to encourage internecine small-scale skirmishes in which local landlords battled for both land and honour.[4] A tournament allowed a nobleman to improve his combat skills in times of peace, with practice fights soon taking place across the continent.[5] Though they were training battles in essence – close to the full horror of war in their earliest forms – the tournaments were soon being regulated. From the late eleventh century onwards, codes of conduct were introduced to rein back the innate violence of the event, with the brutal skills of soldiery transformed into a professionalized sport. This new sport would last – in various forms – through into the seventeenth century.[6]

The move from battle to sport was fairly smooth. Tournaments had begun as little more than a vast melee, a literal free-for-all in which two teams of knights fought each other across an extensive field of play. The word 'tournament' derives from an ancient French verb, 'to whirl about', and early reports suggest that the spectacle was little more than a violent, spinning bundle of bodies, both equine and human.[7] This was not war, however. Death was not the aim. Instead, the capture and ransom of opponents was.[8] By the thirteenth century, however, even the melee was considered too warlike and was replaced by individual jousts. In these contests, the co-ordination of both

horse and lance was facilitated by the introduction of a separating barrier, with risks being further reduced by the blunting
of weapons and the introduction of specialist armour. By now,
the splintering of the lance (and not the man) was the aim of
the game.

Having begun on roaming terrains straddling different
towns, tournaments were also being restricted to licensed venues. Entry fees were imposed and operated as a form of quality
control. With rules and regulations now falling into place – and
given the restricted size of the field, umpires and referees able
to adjudicate – it was looking more and more like sport as we
know it today. We even hear of trumpeting heralds who would
commentate on a match's progress to the delight of the crowd.[9]
By the end of the thirteenth century, therefore, tournaments
had become *the* sporting festival of their day.[10]

Nonetheless, fatalities remained high (though sometimes this
could be due as much to the heat as to the fighting).[11] Sixteen
knights were killed in Saxony in 1179 and 68 killed near
Cologne in 1240, and in 1274 at Châlons-Sur-Marne many
knights were killed in widespread fighting after Edward I of
England was seized in contravention of the rules.[12] It seems
that violence was never far from the surface, often spilling over
into the crowd, something that drew the opprobrium of reign-
ing sovereigns. When Friedrich II licensed one tournament in
1230, he had to appeal to the local populace not to embark on
a campaign of rape, a fact that shows that the levels of violence
in and around this sport were shockingly high.[13]

Despite the alarming levels of violence, contestants were
considered noble. Though the culture of knighthood had developed from humble origins, the social standing of knights had
grown to such an extent by the fifteenth century that even the
most powerful of aristocrats would want to become a knight.
The competitive synthesis of battlefield and playing field had
created a new class of sporting superstar, combining – as one
historian notes – the social standing of polo with the popularity of rugby.[14] But the sport of tourneying also enjoyed a
much broader appeal. Early accounts of the sport describe a

wide range of spectators – sometimes termed 'armchair warriors' – who were not just the great and the good but also identified as the common 'riff-raff' and (even more disparagingly) 'the trash'.[15] As elite and remote as extreme sports today, tourneying was nonetheless genuinely popular. One aspect of the threefold chord certainly repeats.

The combination of social standing and widespread popularity created a spiralling economy of excess, with pomp being piled upon ceremony as mercenary-like professionals toured the circuit with an ever-increasing sense of self-aggrandizement inflated by the crowds. Prize money was increasing to such an extent that tournaments were turning into great displays of local political power, where thousands of knights would gather to compete for weeks on end. A tournament – such as the one at Chauvency in 1280 – would often last a week, with only two days of jousting and a solitary melee.[16] As the lucrative rewards of power increased, the element of theatrical performance grew, with tournaments often incorporating dramatized enactments of ancient codes in which women would be bedecked in dazzling jewels and fine attire as they awarded prizes (sometimes even performing between jousts in erotic, dramatic dance). The tournaments had become spectacles in their own right.

There seems little doubt that a degree of licence surrounded events. Tournaments were usually bracketed with parties, banquets and extravagant festivities, where lavish feasts celebrated the noble honour of contestants amid a painted assembly of dwarfs, giants and allegorical animals emboldened across banners and draped across virgins. In this exotic setting, women would meet their knights in shining armour.[17] Tourneying was definitely romantic.

The sport had developed hand in hand with the culture of chivalry – a word now steeped in romance, though originally derived from the (unflattering) French word for horse. Chivalry was essentially the merging of martial, aristocratic and Christian elements, being heavily influenced by the poetic movement of troubadours from southern France.[18] Soon knights were competing for a lady's honour – and the lady was often the wife of a senior local figure.[19] It means that tournaments and jousts offered the elite an opportunity to display their masculinity before an adoring female populace. The ladies would award all sorts of prizes and tributes to the victorious knights, and genuine questions have to be asked about whether the medieval tournaments attempted to civilize adultery just as much as they civilized war.[20] Whatever the case in point, the 'erotic undercurrent' certainly contributed to the widespread popularity of the tournaments.[21] Not only did they enable feudal allies to prepare for war and provide opportunities for renown, they also allowed knights to win the hand of a lady – sometimes even more. This combination proved extremely popular.[22]

III

The sport of tourneying proved popular despite the vehement opposition of the Church.[23] It is not clear exactly why the Church was so opposed to tourneying, with little evidence of a sustained theological reflection on the character of this sport, though a case can be made from the evidence. The licentious nature of the erotic undercurrents and the brutal nature of the violence must have played their part, especially as the Church has worked so long and hard to protect non-combatants in war through the establishment of both the 'Peace of God' and the 'Truce of God' (two ecclesial mechanisms by which non-combatants and particular days were decreed to be left in peace) – it is clear that tournaments were unquestionably a celebration of the military culture the Church was trying to convert. But evidence suggests the chief cause of opposition was more self-servingly pragmatic: tourneying had gripped popular imagination at the time of the Crusades, and the Church would brook no rival.

The Byzantine Emperor Alexius I Comnenus had petitioned Pope Urban II about the plight of his empire, which was under pressure from waves of Arab attack. The Pope in turn launched a holy war at the Council of Clermont in 1095, calling on

Christian princes to send troops to liberate the Holy Land from Islamic rule. For too long, pilgrims had struggled to reach the holy sites and so knights were promised absolution from their past sins – a papal indulgence that cleared them of all past mistakes – in return for their military service. Many of these Crusaders were deeply devout, expressing their faithful piety through these expeditions; this was a form of penitential warfare characterized by fasting and barefoot marching, just as much as brutal violence.[24] But the get-out-of-jail-free card also fuelled some dubious motives, not least because the invitation was underwritten by the promise of eternal life for knights killed on crusade. This was a win–win situation for some knights. The worst-case scenario was to do what they love in return for an eternal reward.[25] Over the ensuing years, thousands of knights would take the cross and join the Crusades.

The crusading Church saw tournaments as an unwelcome distraction from the good fight. Opposition to them quickly became official, though at first opposition was more ad hoc. Initially, local churches sought only to restrict tourneying to weekends and to ban the holding of tournaments on feast days, though there is plenty of evidence that local clergy were still offering votive masses for competitors and covering events with umbrella blessings, many of which – given the developing culture of chivalry – were Marian in form. But opposition grew in strength and number. Stephen de Fougères, for instance, the Bishop of Rennes, offered a glamourized and idealized vision of knighthood, which looks quite positive at first sight, though it soon becomes clear that the Bishop is using an idealized version to shame the knights of his day. Stephen disparages the realities of dancing, posturing and the luxurious decadence that surrounded the tournaments, recognizing – as one historian puts it – that knights were little more than 'heedless playboys'.[26]

Despite these examples of early criticism, the Church's opposition to tourneying only came to fruition with the launch of the Crusades. The Crusades were seen as the true 'tournament between Heaven and Hell'.[27] In 1130, setting out the ban on tournaments in the Ninth Canon of the Council of Clermont,

Pope Innocent described tournaments as vulgar and detestable, in which the soul was endangered.[28] In the Pope's mind, death in a tournament was never an accident. It was murder or suicide. As a result, anyone killed in tournaments was to be denied a Christian burial, a frightening possibility for the knight and in stark contrast to the papal position on Crusades. A strict ban was therefore put in place, which was repeated and confirmed at the Second Lateran Council in 1139, the Council of Rheims in 1148 and the Third Lateran Council in 1179.[29] Formal ecclesial opposition – universal in scope – lasted through into the fourteenth century.[30]

Though some church leaders had been threatening to excommunicate competitors *before* the Crusades, it is clear that the launching of the Crusades was a game changer.[31] We see this in the pronouncements of many a preacher. Bernard of Clairvaux, for example, was unhappy that some Crusaders wanted to restart tournaments in 1149, describing them – despite their fine silks and armour – as 'impious rogues, sacrilegious thieves, murderers, perjurers and adulterers'. In Bernard's eyes, tournaments were 'accursed' and knights were fighting for the devil.[32]

Ralph Niger – the Canon of Lincoln around 1187 – similarly called on competitors to stop tourneying during the Third Crusade,[33] and, in the mid-thirteenth century, Thomas of Cantimpré goes to great lengths to describe the demonic tribulations of a German knight, while Caesarius of Heisterbach explains that great melees of demons could be seen celebrating in places tournaments had been. This shock-horror approach became quite standard, with demons being heard at the tournament in Neuss in 1241, and the resuscitation of Ralph de Thony's brother – conveyed by the Benedictine monk Matthew Paris – being immediately followed by his confession that he had heard the tortured cries of fallen tourneyers. 'Alas, for those tournaments! Why did I take such joy in them?'[34]

In the fourteenth century, the Dominican John Bromyard castigated contestants and fired off warnings about the hellbound perils of jousting. The fallen are 'martyrs of the devil', hell bound and destined to have their armour nailed to them and to be kissed by insatiable toads.[35] Yet, it was Jacque de Vitry, the Bishop of Acre, who offers the fullest critique. De Vitry levelled the charge that jousting knights were inescapably guilty of committing seven of the deadliest sins. In seeking human praise, they were convicted of *pride*, while the desire for revenge fostered *wrath*. The injured and defeated were liable to *sloth*, whereas the victors would be hamstrung by *avarice* and *gluttony* in their insatiable pursuit of ransoms and feasts. This was compounded by their *envious* desire for earthly reward and their *lecherous* hunting of wanton women. In executive summary, this sport was bad.[36]

It needs to be said that some aspects of the Church's critique were more positive in nature, with preachers regularly recognizing that the tournaments were cultivating a rival pattern of character-forming order, shaping the earthly nobility through the chivalrous virtues of courtesy, pride, honour, largesse, prowess and renown.[37] In effect, this sport was offering a viable alternative to transformation through discipleship and therefore could not be tolerated by the Church. With this in mind, the Church's opposition became more subtle than the scathing, biting and sustained critique of the hell-fire preachers, though on the whole the Church's warnings about tourneying rarely amount to more than the telling of horror stories.[38] But, as bloodthirsty and violent a picture as was painted, it all proved to no avail. Despite the best efforts of the Church – which was helped by secular rulers who saw tourneying as a threat to public order – the sport retained its popularity throughout the ban. And so, with mass disobedience a reality, in 1320, Pope John XXII overturned his predecessor's ban – a ban in which sponsors, contestants and spectators had been threatened with excommunication.

There was little in the way of theological reasoning behind Pope John XXII's U-turn. It was instead pragmatic.[39] Tournaments needed to be rehabilitated, because opposition to them had proved counterproductive. It was reducing the number of knights available for the Crusades, not simply because the existing policy had excommunicated so many knights, but because (obedient) knights were now refusing to travel to the Holy Land, because – with the ban in place – there was nowhere for them to practise their arts. In overturning the ban, Pope John XXII was clearly attempting to *use* the tournaments, sensing that – if harnessed – they could stir up support, both from knights and the wider public, as well as providing a captive audience for collecting money.[40] The logic of Peter du Bois seemed to be compelling: 'Better to ignore the minor sin of tourneying so as to avoid the major catastrophe of failure against the pagans.'[41]

As one historian recognizes, the Church had now come full circle. The Crusades had provided the reason for the tournaments to be banned and now they offered a reason for their vindication. The Church, not sport, had changed its tune.[42] As a result, from the fourteenth century onwards we find the Church permitting this long-since prohibited sport, but only on conditional grounds. Tournaments were not to be celebrated as a good in themselves – not something simply to enjoy – but were instead set to serve a different purpose: preparation for the Crusades. The Church therefore attempted to redefine the culture of knighthood into its own image, not least in continuing to map the monastic vow of chastity on to the ascetic obligations of the Templars and Hospitallers (two quasi-religious orders vowed to the protection of pilgrims in Jerusalem).[43] But here the self-interest of the Church had led to its full capitulation.[44] Tournaments – in their high pageantry and culture of chivalry – began to mark public life such as diplomatic meetings and the like, as well as religious events such as marriages and coronations. Time and again, pre-joust masses were said and blessings offered to good effect.[45] Some Christians even began to cast tourneying in a very bright light indeed, with Christ himself being portrayed as a tourneyer in *William's Vision of Piers Plowman*.[46] The Church's capitulation was complete, however, when jousts took place in St Peter's Square in 1471. Sport was again to be found right at the heart of religion.[47]

IV

All in all, it would seem that tournaments proved irrepressible to the medieval Church and – as one historian puts it – the Church learned that 'fashion and fun were stronger than censure'.[48] As a result, with the Church embracing the tournaments, we can see that our threefold pattern is in place. First, sport – despite the very best efforts of both Church and State – remained deeply popular throughout this period. It was impossible to erase it despite the best threats of kings and popes. Second, the Church is again (almost naturally) opposed to this sport, finding all sorts of problems in it and essentially seeing it as a rival. Whether it is because sport offers a false order of knightly formation-in-virtue or is an unwanted distraction from the Crusades, sport is an obstacle to the true worship of the Christian and an impediment to the religious life. Finally, with the popularity outlasting censure, the Church seeks to accommodate sport into its life, essentially co-opting it to its own purposes, *using* it by harnessing it to its mission and drawing it into the centre of its life. Uneasy as this proved in practice, the Church sought some sort of partnership. Here, in the medieval period, we therefore find striking similarities to the early Church's view of sport. The threefold chord of popularity, opposition and instrumental use resounds.

Notes

1 As indicated in the previous chapter, the relationship between the Christian faith, Roman life and the conversion of Constantine is much more complex than I can do justice to here. Nonetheless, the general point remains: the Church's position changed dramatically (even if in slow motion). For an excellent account of the complexities of the period after Constantine, see Peter Brown, *Through the Eye of a Needle: Wealth, the Fall of Rome and the Making of Christianity in the West, 350–550 AD*, Princeton, NJ: Princeton University Press, 2012.

2 For a helpful – and beautifully illustrated – survey of the colourful spectacle of medieval knights, see Richard Barber and Juliet Barker, *Tournaments: Jousts, Chivalry and Pageants in the Middle Ages*, Woodbridge: Boydell Press, 2000.

3 Barber and Barker, *Tournaments*, p. 27.

4 The wars between the houses of Blois and Anjou in Touraine are a good example. Maurice Keen, *Chivalry*, New Haven, CT and London: Yale University Press, 2005, pp. 23–30.

5 They allowed soldiers to familiarize themselves with contemporary innovations in technical equipment such as stirrups, saddles and the new forms of lances.

6 Some commentators have likened the transformation of soldiery into a sport to modern yacht racing, which is now adrift from its naval origins and instead a highly stylized event with little practical application. Tournaments should be considered likewise, cut adrift from their military origins. Barber and Barker, *Tournaments*, p. 4.

7 David Crouch, *Tournament*, London and New York: Hambledon and Continuum, 2005, p. 3.

8 Crouch, *Tournament*, p. 151.

9 Crouch, *Tournament*, pp. 63–5.

10 Keen, *Chivalry*, pp. 86–7.

11 Keen, *Chivalry*, p. 87. It is also clear that many notable people died. In 1216, Geoffrey de Mandeville, the Earl of Essex, was killed at a tournament.

12 Allen Guttmann, *Sports: The First Five Millennia*, Amherst and Boston, MA: University of Massachusetts Press, 2004, p. 52.

13 Guttmann, *Sports*, p. 53.

14 Crouch, *Tournament*, p. 19.

15 Crouch, *Tournament*, pp. 55–6.

16 Keen, *Chivalry*, p. 87.

17 See Shirl James Hoffman, *Good Game: Christianity and the Culture of Sports*, Waco, TX: Baylor University Press, 2010, p. 51.

18 Keen, *Chivalry*, p. 16.

19 On the place of women in tournament culture, see Crouch, *Tournament*, pp. 156–9.

20 Sometimes this questionable aspect is revealed in the punishment of adulterers rather than the recording of scandalous facts. See Barber and Barker, *Tournaments*, p. 9.

21 Keen, *Chivalry*, p. 91.

22 Knights would be – at a minimum – garnished in the tokens, sleeves and the locks of hair of the honoured ladies. See Keen, *Chivalry*, pp. 88–91.

23 Keen argues that tournaments continued 'in spite of the church's disapproval' and 'consistent censure'. Keen, *Chivalry*, p. 83. For a good summary of the Church's opposition, see Barber and Barker, *Tournaments*, pp. 139–49.

24 The pious nature of the Crusaders, and the penitential nature of their warfare, is a major theme in Jonathan Riley-Smith, *The Crusades, Christianity and Islam*, New York: University of Columbia Press, 2008. This book explodes many popular myths about the Crusades.

25 Keen, *Chivalry*, pp. 44–5.

26 David Crouch, *The Image of Aristocracy in Britain: 1000–1300*, London: Routledge, 1992, p. 139.

27 Crouch, *The Image of Aristocracy in Britain*, p. 135.

28 Keen, *Chivalry*, p. 84.

29 Barber and Barker, *Tournaments*, p. 17.

30 The ban was finally lifted by Pope John XXII in 1316. See Richard Kaeuper, *Chivalry and Violence in Medieval Europe*, new edn, Oxford: Oxford University Press, 2001, p. 80.

31 For example, Archbishop Wichman of Magdeburg was busy excommunicating before the Crusades. Crouch, *Tournament*, p. 10.

32 Kaeuper, *Chivalry and Violence in Medieval Europe*, pp. 76–80; see also Barber and Barker, *Tournaments*, p. 140, for St Bernard of Clairvaux's view.

33 Crouch, *Tournament*, p. 141.

34 Keen, *Chivalry*, pp. 94–5.

35 Richard W. Kaeuper, *Holy Warriors: The Religious Ideology of Chivalry*, Philadelphia, PA: University of Pennsylvania Press, 2009, p. 68; see also Barber and Barker, *Tournaments*, p. 144.

36 Keen, *Chivalry*, p. 95.

37 Note: despite ecclesial ban and no genuine rival – Islam excepted – sport still morphed into the pseudo-rival religion of chivalrous knighthood. See Keen, *Chivalry*, pp. 99–100.

38 Barber and Barker, *Tournaments*, p. 144.

39 Pope John XXII is here 'bowing to the inevitable' according to Barber and Barker. See Barber and Barker, *Tournaments*, p. 141.

40 Hoffman, *Good Game*, p. 53.

41 Barber and Barker, *Tournaments*, p. 141.

42 Barber and Barker, *Tournaments*, p. 145.

43 Keen, *Chivalry*, pp. 49–55.

44 Hoffman, *Good Game*, p. 55.

45 Barber and Barker, *Tournaments*, pp. 166–73.

46 Barber and Barker, *Tournaments*, p. 145.

47 Guttmann, *Sports*, p. 53.

48 Crouch, *The Image of Aristocracy in Britain*, p. 135.

5

Case Study (II): Sport, Puritans and Muscular Christians

Today, if a person is opposed to some form of fun, they can be dismissed as a puritan. This often derogatory term implies that the person in question thinks pleasure is bad, a judgement that is usually based on their religious principles. The term 'puritan' in fact stems from a group of English Protestants from the late sixteenth and seventeenth centuries, many of whom were Calvinists. The Reformation had fragmented the medieval Church, creating a snowballing mass of protest and opposition to ecclesial corruption and malpractice that spread right across Europe. In England, events were locally shaped by the powerful idiosyncrasies of Henry VIII, with the eventual split from Rome producing – through widespread trial and turmoil – a dynamic via media that sought to harness both Catholic practice and Protestant ideals in a positive compromise. The Puritans, however, felt that the English Reformation had not run its course. Life in the newly established church was far too complicated. The English Puritans wanted to purify Christianity by simplifying things.

The Puritan way of life was quite distinct. Heavily influenced by strands in Calvinist theology, they believed that a limited number of people were predestined for salvation, with everyone else heading towards eternal damnation. Though no one could know if they themselves were part of the lucky Elect, the hidden secret of their destiny would be revealed in their daily life. From a Puritan perspective, therefore, time on earth will be defined by hard, honest work and simple, sober living. As this suggests, life was not much fun. It was a very serious business. Even Christmas – at least in the Plymouth Colony of New England – was to be banned.[1]

With this strict work ethic in mind, it will come as no surprise that the Puritans were not great fans of sport, though their approach is more complex than might at first be suspected. John Bunyan – the famous author of *Pilgrim's Progress* – gives us an insight into their views, though appropriately the path away from Bunyan twists and turns in all sorts of directions. Bunyan was ashamed of many things that he had done before his conversion, not least the many years he spent dancing and bell-ringing! But in Bunyan's mind, sport held a special place. This was because God had saved him from it, quite literally. One Sunday on Elstow Village Green, Bunyan had been playing a game called tip-cat. Tip-cat bears a strong family resemblance to modern games such as cricket and baseball in that it involves – from what we know – hitting an object as far as possible without getting caught. As Bunyan played the game, he heard the Lord Jesus Christ call out to him, 'Will you leave your sins behind and go to heaven or have your sins and go to hell?' For Bunyan the implications were as obvious as the answer was clear. Recreational sport is a sin and it leads to hell. He decided to have no more to do with it.[2]

Fuelled with this knowledge, Bunyan set about his work, embracing the serious, hard-working way of life advocated by the Puritans. Joining their growing ranks, Bunyan began to preach the gospel amid trials and imprisonments in one of the most turbulent periods in English history. But with England restoring a form of Catholicism under Charles II, the Puritans were again being threatened with persecution.[3] They had already begun to emigrate in large numbers by this time, setting sail towards the 'new' territories of North America, with the New World offering the Puritans an opportunity to live a properly Christian life. The Plymouth Colony and Massachusetts Bay had been established by 1630, with their self-regulating society being self-consciously ordered towards the Lordship of Jesus Christ. Left to their own devices – and working on a blank canvas – the Puritans were free to handle sport in whatever way they liked.

It is clear that the American Puritans did have a well-defined vision of the good life, one which was spelled out in the writings of their leader John Winthrop who detailed a theocratic 'city on a hill'.[4] Underlining the precious nature of time and the opportunity for valuable work – as Benjamin Franklin soon argued, time is money – Winthrop argued that God would bless the new community if everyone in it lived a hard-working life, one that was properly ordered towards the Sabbath. At first, sport was acceptable (just about). Winthrop himself recognized what he called 'due recreation', which he saw as part of a properly governed life, though he certainly acknowledged that there were dangers, arguing that recreation can be a distraction from the primary task of being in continuous conversation with heaven.[5] But Winthrop acknowledged (somewhat reluctantly) that life without sport would be 'melancholick and uncomfortable'.[6] He himself found abstinence counterproductive, becoming increasingly distracted in his devotions instead of more and more focused. As a result, he returned to his moderate workouts, thereby finding himself 'much refreshed'. As Winthrop saw it, exercise could help the Christian live a life dedicated to God. It could be of use to the Christian.

This instrumental view of exercise was being echoed back across the Atlantic, with the English Puritan Richard Baxter making a similar point in his *Christian Directory*. In Baxter's view, vice only gets a foothold when physical pleasure becomes its own end, but if exercise is set to serve a higher purpose, fun can be tolerated.[7] The Englishman John Downame – another important influence on Puritan thought – found a positive place for sport in his theology. Writing in his seventeenth-century *Guide to Godlynesse*, he argued that sport is beneficial to the participants even though it was of 'the basest calling', akin to eating and drinking.[8] Downame argued that it is 'refreshing' and punctuates fatigue, boredom and dutiful hard labour, a tonic for people amid the drudgery of their true calling.[9]

Protestant Christians – both in America and England – were discovering a potential use for sport.

With Christians identifying positive uses for sport, they soon began exploring how it can be used in society, not least in preparing soldiers for battle, as well as socializing their citizens through the practice of teamwork. Puritan writers can be found celebrating the benefits of sports such as swimming and bowling, and the officials at Harvard College – founded in the Massachusetts Bay Colony in 1636 – decided to include a couple of hours of exercise in their students' week.[10] The underlying logic was clear: exercise makes men happy; a happy man functions more efficiently; and efficiency is good for the community, because better work brings God's blessing. Sport could serve the Christian life.

We can see what has happened here. The Puritan community had begun to subsume recreational sports into their work ethic, setting it to serve within the effort-driven economy of divine blessing. But, at precisely the same time, they were also struggling with sport.[11] The wider question of Sabbath observance was the main problem. In America, for example, the elected Magistrates – who governed Puritan society – understood their primary role as making the Sabbath *holy*. Citizens were therefore to be punished for all manner of breaches to the Sabbath code, even to the extent of being imprisoned if they did not go to church. Sport of course – in its distinction from work – was played mainly on the Sabbath, and so it caught the eye of the Magistrates, not least because of its association with a secondary culture of drinking and gambling.[12] Constables were therefore set loose, searching for any signs of 'gaming, singing and dancing',[13] and, by the mid-seventeenth century, the Magistrates were calling a halt to a full range of sports.[14] The General Court now outlawed bowling, for instance, and in Boston we find the council banning football from the streets, lanes and enclosures of the town. By the late seventeenth century, this ban had been extended to horseracing and cockfighting,[15] with law after law being introduced to protect Sabbath observance by banning 'any Game, Sport, Play or Recreation'.

'An Act for the Better Observation and Keeping of the Lords-Day' was published at least four times in less than forty years at this time, and warned against the playing of sports.[16] Useful though it be, sport was nowhere near being celebrated. Instead, it was judged more trouble than it was worth.[17]

II

But times were changing. In the eighteenth century, an evangelical revival began to sweep through churches on both sides of the Atlantic. Though the revival drew deeply from Puritan thinking, it moved away from its roots by re-establishing a strong link between holiness and happiness, not least in the joyful celebration of God's immediate presence in worship. Jonathan Edwards – the American theologian – had helped to rehabilitate the affections and emotions into the Christian life, recognizing that 'the human capacity for pleasure was not just the province of the sinful passions: it was part of the spiritual nature' as well.[18] By the nineteenth century, some of the more radical leaders in Britain – such as Edward Irving and Samuel Earnshaw – had built on Edwards' foundation and were beginning to argue that Puritan opposition to fun proved counterproductive. Abstinence had become a sin in being a form of pious works-righteousness.[19]

In many ways, the point was simple. The Puritanical strand in Christian piety had (inadvertently) handed too much power to fun, mistakenly creating a competitive zero-sum structure in which fun became an equal and opposite force to piety.[20] In doing so, Christians had created a rod for their own back, haemorrhaging young people from their churches because they wanted to live rather than suffer the boredom of the Christian life.[21] Thomas Chalmers – the most eminent leader in the Scottish church – had begun to preach that legalism was more pernicious than antinomianism, the Puritan cure worse than the sporting disease, and, with the sterile religiosity of Puritanism now being spelled out, fun was seen as fertile soil for the gospel.[22] As Revd Rowland Hill asked, 'Why should the devil have all the good tunes?'[23]

In this changing climate, it was only a matter of time before people argued that pleasure could be controlled by sport, a move that prepared the soil for a new muscular form of Christianity.[24] The movement of Muscular Christianity was an attempt to re-imagine the body as 'a vehicle of virtue'.[25] The early leaders – people like Charles Kingsley – argued that some virtues could not be learned through study, but they could be learned through the body. Endurance, temper, self-restraint, fairness, daring and honour, for example – 'the give and take of life' – could be learned physically, through the 'charm of play'.[26] The author Thomas Hughes made the point forcefully in his most influential work, *Tom Brown's Schooldays*. Hughes' book stimulated a process of radical re-imagination, in which sport was seen as a way in which young men could be socialized, learning virtue in action.

In next to no time at all, Christians were moving away from the Puritan stance and beginning to welcome sport into their common life. Opposition was becoming embrace. Schools made the first move, with the first gym opening at Uppingham in 1860. Soon parish churches followed suit. In 1879, for example, St Andrew's Fulham Fields formed a Christian cricket and football club for young boys, which – over time – grew and transformed into Fulham FC, a professional club now playing football in the English Premier League.[27] This was a symbol of an underlying attempt to get the moral and physical virtues to merge, a move based on some simple theological insights, such as those found in Thomas Hughes' *The Manliness of Christ*, where Jesus is re-presented as the courageous hero of perseverance, a man fit to emulate.[28] This shift to moral physicality/physical morality was most evident in the YMCA, which had begun life by denouncing sport but was now beginning to embrace it more fully. By 1876, the YMCA incorporated its first gym into its London premises.[29] Membership soon rocketed, and the new buildings became 'virtual temples to sport'.[30]

With Christian movements creating genuine sporting clubs, the Church appeared to be heading in a new direction. Sport had become a mediator between pleasure and holiness,[31] a means to betterment – 'a rival account of salvation' even[32] – with physical discipline, self-control and temperance being linked to physical health and the well-being of the soul.[33] What was happening was that play was effectively being turned into work. The Protestant work ethic had extended into sport: sport can improve you, it can build character and inculcate virtue; and just so: sport can become the vehicle of salvation, its physicality a new brand of Christian piety, and therein a new form of works righteousness.[34] As one commentator argues, 'the project seemed to boil down to an assertion that manliness *is* godliness'.[35] Sport was no longer opposed. Puritanism was instead.

But there was a sting in the tail. As sport became a conduit for salvation, the traditional practices of the spiritual life became increasingly redundant. Who needs prayer, Bible study and fasting, if you can live the good life by playing cricket? As the YMCA discovered, membership grew – but only among the gym-using associate members; Bible study, in contrast, plummeted.[36] It looked like Christians – in naturalizing the supernatural – were in danger of sawing off the branch they were sitting on. Churches were now in danger of becoming sporting clubs. It seems they had forgotten the danger of sport and the way it can lead Christians away from a life with Christ. This is precisely what the Church had opposed in the first place.

III

Let us now take a step back and survey the way in which the Church – strung across time – has engaged with sport over the centuries.[37] We have seen that history is quite messy, resisting simplistic caricature and instead resembling a complex maze of interactions in which equal and opposite forces seem to be pulling in two directions at once. Nonetheless, three notes have been identified in different settings. First, from the earliest days of the Church, through medieval papacies and on into evangelical piety, Christians have struggled with sport. Sport has been opposed and denounced at regular intervals from pulpits, Councils and imperial thrones. Sometimes seen as a distraction from true discipleship, sometimes identified as a lethal idolatrous practice, the Church has argued that all manner of sin lurks within it: false sacrifice, gambling, pride, vanity, prowess and the like, a litany of vice from which Christians must flee whether they are in ancient Rome, medieval France or the territories of New England. The Church denounces and separates. Sport is dangerous in the Christian life.

Second, we have seen that the Church – even at the height of its powers – never quite manages to erase sport from the life of the community. Sport, it seems, is unstoppably popular. Third, in recognizing the popularity of sport, we have seen that the Church has often had to embrace it, essentially trying to find a use for it, often missionary, sometimes soteriological, though regularly little more than a recognition that games are better for the masses than drinking and fighting. Accepted only conditionally, the immovable object of sport is harnessed to the Christian mission. Sport is used.

Though history is kaleidoscopic and complex, it can teach us this much. Though the balance between the three notes varies – sometimes more opposition, sometimes more use, invariably popular – the three notes simultaneously sound out. This historical chord is therefore the background noise within which we must do our thinking. We need to wrestle with the question of sport in a way that honours this history – at least in the sense of understanding it, explaining it, and judging whether the Church's dual approach of opposition and use is the best way to handle this unstoppably popular activity. This is the task to which we turn. It is time for us to begin our theological analysis of sport. Our historical soundings end.

Notes

1 In the Puritan mind, God gives each person a certain number of days. Any time wasted for no good reason was 'an illegal draft on one's account of God-given hours and minutes'. Shirl James Hoffman, *Good Game: Christianity and the Culture of Sports*, Waco, TX: Baylor University Press, 2010, p. 78.

2 Hoffman, *Good Game*, p. 85.

3 In England, as far back as 1618, James I had sought to stem Puritan hostility to sport with the publication of the *Book of Sports*, in which popular amusements were protected (though the book – during the Long Parliament – had been publicly burnt by the Puritans). See Steven J. Overman, *The Protestant Ethic and the Spirit of Sport*, Macon, GA: Mercer University Press, 2011, p. 34.

4 For this, see Nancy Struna, 'Puritans and Sport: The Irretrievable Tide of Change', *Journal of Sport History* 4.1 (1977), pp. 1–21.

5 Overman, *Protestant Ethic and the Spirit of Sport*, p. 38.

6 Cited in Struna, 'Puritans and Sport', p. 3.

7 Overman, *Protestant Ethic and the Spirit of Sport*, p. 32.

8 Cited in Struna, 'Puritans and Sport', p. 2.

9 See *The Christian Warfare*, cited in Struna, 'Puritans and Sport', p. 3.

10 See Harvard College Records, 3 vols, Boston, MA: Publications of the Colonial Society of Massachusetts, 1935, III, 330–33, cited in Struna, 'Puritans and Sport', p. 9.

11 See Overman, *Protestant Ethic and the Spirit of Sport*, pp. 35ff.

12 Though sport was useful in instilling discipline, the Puritans recognized that it attracted an unruly crowd. Control and prohibition followed. In 1709, the Puritan leader Increase Mather offered his *Advice to a Young Man*. Mather advocates lawful, moderate sport, but rails against indulgence in 'sinful sports and pastimes'. Increase Mather, 'Advice to a Young Man', Boston, 1709, p. 28, cited in Struna, 'Puritans and Sport', p. 16. By the 1830s and 1840s, powerful voices had aligned across the Atlantic: Wesley, Wilberforce and Baxter were all railing against *pleasure*. Cf. Dominic Erdozain, 'In Praise of Folly: Sport as Play', *Anvil* 28.1 (2012), pp. 20–34.

13 See Massachusetts Records, II, 70, p. 180, cited in Struna, 'Puritans and Sport', p. 5.

14 See Massachusetts Records, IV, part I, Aug 30, 1653, pp. 150–1, cited in Struna, 'Puritans and Sport', p. 8.

15 'Second Report of the Boston Records Commissioners', in *The Memorial History of Boston, 1630–1880*, ed. Justin Windsor, Boston, MA: James R. Osgood, 1880, p. 229, cited in Struna, 'Puritans and Sport', p. 11, and for horseracing, *Massachusetts Court of Assistants Records, 1630–1692*, 3 vols, Boston, MA: County of Suffolk, 1901, II, April 9, 1672, cited in Struna, 'Puritans and Sport', p. 11.

16 Struna, 'Puritans and Sport'.

17 Nonetheless, there is something else we should note here. Sport remained popular. The Puritans never managed to quash sports entirely, with one historical commentator concluding that 'objectionable forms of recreation' continued

among their own people. Sport – as we might by now expect – proved resilient, even in the hostile environment of Puritan society. Overman, *Protestant Ethic and the Spirit of Sport*, pp. 37ff.

18 Dominic Erdozain, *The Problem of Pleasure: Sport, Recreation and the Crisis of Victorian Religion*, Woodbridge: Boydell, 2010, p. 56. My deep debt to Erdozain's work will be evident in what follows.

19 Irving argued that separation from 'sports and amusements of the fields' was 'bondage'. Erdozain, *Problem of Pleasure*, p. 82.

20 Pleasure was given centre stage in a cosmic drama, and by being over critiqued it was in fact overvalued. See Erdozain, *Problem of Pleasure*, p. 76.

21 Erdozain, 'In Praise of Folly'.

22 See Erdozain, *Problem of Pleasure*, pp. 80–2.

23 Quoted in Erdozain, *Problem of Pleasure*, p. 57.

24 Erdozain, 'In Praise of Folly'.

25 Erdozain, 'In Praise of Folly'.

26 Erdozain, *Problem of Pleasure*, p. 99.

27 Many professional teams today share similar ecclesial roots. See Peter Lupson, *Thank God for Football: The Illustrated Companion*, London: SPCK, 2010. I mention St Andrew's as I have the delight of being Associate Priest to the people there.

28 Erdozain, *Problem of Pleasure*, pp. 105–6.

29 Erdozain, *Problem of Pleasure*, pp. 172–3.

30 Erdozain, *Problem of Pleasure*, p. 184.

31 See this working itself out in the YMCA. Erdozain, *Problem of Pleasure*, p. 180.

32 Erdozain, *Problem of Pleasure*, p. 86.

33 Erdozain, 'In Praise of Folly'.

34 Dominic Erdozain argues that the term 'Muscular Christianity' reveals the absurdity of the idea, saying we might as well have 'mystical railways'. Erdozain, *Problem of Pleasure*, p. 99.

35 Erdozain, *Problem of Pleasure*, p. 103.

36 Erdozain, *Problem of Pleasure*, pp. 221–9.

37 With a very close eye on the Victorian age in England, Erdozain helpfully identifies five approaches to sport in the Church at the end of the nineteenth century. Erdozain, *Problem of Pleasure*, pp. 157–61:

1 Separate and denounce.
2 Look on the world as a place rightfully to be enjoyed.
3 Use sport for conversion and the 'retention of the young'.
4 Embrace sport as the possessor of moral and spiritual properties.
5 Regard recreation *as* religion.

PART 2

Analytic Soundings

6

Notes on Sport: A Working Definition

In the first part of this book, we examined how the Church has engaged with sport in the past. We set about this task fairly confidently, proceeding as if we knew what we were talking about. We never once stopped to explain what sport exactly *is*, never moving beyond the assumption that I-know-it-when-I-see-it. This deficit must now be addressed. We must attempt to say what sport precisely is. That – to recall – is the stated aim of the book.

We therefore begin a sustained analysis of sport. First, we will move towards a working definition by drawing on the work of philosophers, sociologists and cultural historians. Having drawn from their written work, we will inquire how the working definition can be developed theologically. We will do this by first excavating Christian teaching on God's creative action, to come up with a constructive proposal about the nature of the world. We will then use this theological proposal to define what we are doing when we play (or watch) sport.

This theological definition will help us understand why sport is so unstoppably popular, as well as enable us to judge whether or not the Church – on the basis of its own belief in God – needs to adopt a new posture towards sport or continue with its old habits of opposition and use. Readers will thereby discover whether sport should have a place in the Christian life, and, if so, what sort of place it should be. Finally, the explanatory power of the thesis will be harnessed to explore a number of pressing issues in contemporary sport. We will look at questions such as the nature of competition and the professionalization of modern sport. For now, however, we begin our initial analysis with a simple question: *what is sport?* A provisional answer to this question is the work of this chapter.

II

What then is sport? To approach an answer to this question, we first offer a working definition. Definitions usually identify a subject, often by pinpointing its basic qualities. We do this by locating the subject first in a wider category before specifying its distinguishing features. If we were trying to define a chair, for instance, we might say that a chair is a piece of *furniture* (the broader category) before specifying that *a person sits on it* (the distinguishing feature). Thus we would have defined a chair as *a piece of furniture someone sits on.* That said, this initial definition might not be the final word on the subject. We might want to add something about a chair needing to have a back (to distinguish it from a stool), and it being designed for only one person to sit on (to distinguish it from a sofa). We might even want to say that it is part of the created order (to distinguish it from God). Our substantive point, however, is simple. Though the initial definition need not be the final word, it remains a good place to start. We therefore adopt this approach as we look to define sport: broad category, then distinguishing features.

Into what broader category does sport fit? The obvious answer is that sport is a type of *play*.[1] Of course, sport can be work, not only in the physical effort invested but also in the financial rewards received. This is something we will need to look at in a later chapter. Nevertheless, we kick off with the commonplace observation: we *play* sport.[2] But what exactly does this mean?

Chances are, everyone will have played at some stage in their lives. In fact, it is hard to imagine how anyone could live long in this world without – to some extent or other – playing. Play therefore can be seen as an unavoidable aspect to life, similar to eating, drinking and sleeping in that everyone will do it. But – familiar though it is – when we stop to think about it, we quickly discover that play, like all the most basic realities in life, is quite difficult to define. Even the greatest minds wrestling with the question have struggled to pin it down completely. Their answers, however, do share a lot in common. They will help us get a foothold in the subject.

Many analysts believe that play is a *natural activity*. It is thought to be natural, because animals – as well as humans – appear to play. We see television footage of animals, such as lion cubs, monkeys and acrobatic dolphins, playing amid exotic landscapes, and – much closer to home – we will have seen dogs and cats at play. We might not believe that every animal plays (think of fish, birds and workaholic ants), but the fact remains that some animals appear to play.[3] To many an analyst, this indicates that we are dealing here with a natural activity.

Because play appears to be natural, many theorists have joined up the dots and argued that it is serving a biological purpose. It is sometimes described as the way the young are trained, honing and sharpening their instincts by modelling future scenarios. Think of play fighting, for instance. Others have argued that it is how our excess energy is discharged, effectively functioning as a safety valve through which pent-up emotions are exhaled. If we did not let off steam we would soon – like a steam train – explode, our health would be damaged (as Aristotle argued) or subconscious conflicts remain unresolved (as Freud claimed).[4] Whatever the precise outcome, all such accounts share something in common: play is set to serve biology; it is a functional mechanism within our personal biosphere.

Despite the popularity of these biological accounts, many writers identify a serious problem within them. Johan Huizinga – a Dutch historian – put his finger on the problem, arguing that a biological account makes the mistake of setting play to serve something that is not play, and – in so doing – misses the most important quality of play, it is *fun*.[5] Huizinga goes on to argue that fun is somehow related to *freedom*.[6] It is easy to see what Huizinga means by this. Many things are unavoidable in life. We have to eat, we have to drink and we have to sleep, for instance. If we decided not to do these things then we would be in trouble, our lives would be at risk. That is fairly obvious. Play, however, is a little different. If we did not play, we would not be overwhelmed in quite the same way. Hunger, thirst or tiredness would not strike us. This makes play tangibly different from activities such as eating, drinking or sleeping. While those most basic components to life are necessary, play in contrast is not. No one needs to do it.[7]

Put otherwise, when we play we choose to play. This all seems fairly obvious when we think of it. Though someone – for better or worse – can be forced to eat or drink (think intravenous drip) or even forced to sleep (think knockout punch), it is much harder to imagine how someone could be forced to play. Of course, we know that someone can be compelled to join in with a game. Many a schoolchild will testify to this. Peer pressure and compulsory classes are genuine realities. But we also know that there is something quite wrong with this approach. Forced play is not play. It is at best simulating play. This makes it quite different from eating, drinking and sleeping. When someone is forced to eat, drink or sleep, they are still genuinely eating, drinking and sleeping. But if someone is forced to play, they are not really playing. They are instead caught up in a lie. In effect, an essential quality is lost through compulsion.[8] Put more positively, play is – by its nature – an expression of freedom.

The irreducibly free nature of play makes it qualitatively different from all the responsibilities people have in life. People have to catch buses to go to work to earn money to pay for food to eat to survive. Though there is some degree of choice in the matter – they might instead walk to the cash machine to draw from their inherited trust fund, or wander to the bottom of the garden to pick an apple from a tree – these sorts of activities are work, because they have to be done.[9] Play, in contrast, is different. 'We don't expect our games to feed or clothe or shelter us.'[10]

The word 'sport' in fact suggests this. Though the etymological link is lost to sight today, 'sport' is derived from 'disport', which in turn is formed from 'to carry' (*portare*) and 'apart' (*dis-*).[11] When we play we carry ourselves apart from the necessary activities of our existence. To play, therefore, is to enter a very different sphere of everyday life. This explains why we work so hard to set it apart. Think only of a playtime. By creating a special time for children to play, play is distinguished from their schoolwork. Play is extra-curricular, the children are dis-ported away from the forced lessons and the labour of learning. It is a special time where the children get to do what they want. They are miles from the serious business of schooling. It is playtime, the 'world of freedom'.[12]

And time is not the only way in which we distinguish play. It can also be set apart *spatially*. Through explicit sign and symbol – perhaps by marking out lines to create a pitch, a court or a track – we set out a distinct area which becomes the field of play, a play*ground*. This space can then be complemented by additional symbols such as costumes, uniforms or kits, which combine to emphasize that something quite different is going on here.[13] Taken together, playtime and playground function as 'parentheses' that bracket out everyday life; they suspend the ordinary world.[14]

Things are not always so obvious. Sometimes – such as when a group of children play make-believe pirates or pretend to be princesses – the distinction between play and the rest of life is harder to see. The game is demarcated only by an unspoken 'imagine as if'.[15] But the point here is that *something* will be setting play apart from everything else, signifying and actualizing that something quite different is going on here. Play is a set-apart sphere of freedom.

Huizinga uses the language of 'bounding' to describe what we are doing when we demarcate play. Bounding is a process that creates what Roger Caillois – a French sociologist – describes as a 'pure space'.[16] This pure space, however, is never a vacuum. It is not an empty nothingness, so to speak, stripped of all form, abandoned to chaos. It is instead positive in shape, its features being determined by an internal ordering, a prearranged set of set-apart rules, which the participants must embrace in order to establish the arena of play. We cannot have un-ruled space. Space is determined (otherwise it is not space) and determination is ordered. Thus the bounded space must be rule governed. Play is freely *determined*.

The logical consequence of this position is that if someone wants to play, they must play by the rules.[17] If they do not play by the rules, it is not that they are bad at the game. It is instead that they are outside the game – they are not actually playing in the space provided.[18] They may be an inexperienced novice or instead a wily old cheat, but either way – by not playing by the rules – the person is destroying the game. Play, we might say, is threatened as much by chaos as it is by coercion. This means that to play is to enter a 'weirdly coherent parallel universe', as the Cambridge philosopher Steven Conner puts it, in which the rules of the game create a positive space that is set apart from the day-to-day ordering of life.[19] It is to enter 'a second reality', and – paradoxically – this second reality must be taken seriously.[20] The metarule – as Conner shows – is that we must try to win. We must not 'play at playing'. Fun (paradoxically) is a serious business.[21]

To play is therefore to submit unnecessarily to the absolute necessity of the rules. It is to reject chaos just as much as it is to reject compulsion. It is neither a lawless vacuum nor an unavoidable necessity. It is a *contingent order of freedom*. This means, however, that the rules of the game – as necessary as they are to play – are never necessary when viewed from the outside. If they were, we would not be playing freely. There simply is no reason why the ball is allowed to bounce only once in tennis or why three teams do not play each other at football or why the stone must skip when skimming across a lake. It is not necessary in that sense. Things could be different. To this extent, therefore, we can say that the rules of the game are arbitrary.

But we must avoid a common misunderstanding here. The arbitrary nature of the rules does not make them pointless. Of course, from the outside it is easy to question the point of a game. Why would someone spend all day at a cricket match trying to hit an arbitrary target, be that stumps or ball? Or why would someone try to crunch their way through a wall of brutal opponents to get an odd-shaped ball into the endzone? With no obvious reason for an outsider to see, it is easy to question the point of the game. Games look ludicrous. But as appropriate as the word is – cf. Latin *ludere*, to play – games are not ludicrous.[22] There may be no obvious reason why things are as they are, but this does not make the game pointless. Games – to state the obvious in some cases – do have points. An object, such as a ball, is not aimed anywhere, a simple shooting at the sky. Instead the object is aimed *at* something (a tennis ball at the opposing half of the court, a basketball at the hoop, an arrow at the target).[23] The point may be internal, but it remains a point.

This is another way of saying that the game only makes sense within itself. This is why we do not like it when someone suddenly asks 'Would it not be more efficient for everyone to use their hands as well as their feet?' This person will either have invented a new game or be asking a stupid question for a footballer/soccer player. There *is* no reason why the outfield players cannot use their hands, other than the simple reason that it is not part of the freely determined contingent meaning that *is* football. But to play soccer, they *must* abide by this rule. It forms part of the point of the game.[24] Likewise it looks ridiculous to hide when you are neither in danger nor trying to ambush someone. But if you are playing a game of hide-and-seek any attempt to justify the fact you are hiding will spoil the game itself. Unnecessary, externally worthless and pointless they may appear, but any game – as Conner recognizes – is a strange yet coherent parallel rule-bound universe into which we choose to be freely dis-ported.

In fact, if anyone questions whether it is worth playing a game they are (quite literally) a *spoilsport*, because there is no external measure or motivation by which to rationalize the game.[25] All of this is to say that a game – contra biological theories – cannot be made sense of by setting it to serve an outside purpose. A game is not pragmatic in this sense. The goal is part of the game, not beyond it.

This freely determined, contingent and self-contained nature of play means that – as widely recognized – it is 'superfluous', as Huizinga puts it.[26] Because it serves nothing outside itself, play is very different from other aspects of our life, a point Caillois is keen to underline through a series of negatives. Caillois argues that a defining feature of play is that nothing is created. When the final whistle blows, there is no gathering of the harvest or distribution of the produce. There may be an internal economy – a points system perhaps, even a trophy – but nothing is created by the game. There is no beautiful painting or valuable vase as with art, and no car or positive balance sheet as with industry. The game is simply the game. It is radically non-productive, a passing event in which time, energy and skill are invested for no apparent reason. Therefore, playing is a strange economy of gratuitous waste. It is barren. It is *for nothing*.[27]

This claim is quite provocative. It is also easily misunderstood. Philosophers do not deny there are consequences to play – it is not an absolutely parallel universe, completely disconnected from the rest of life. Play therefore *can* bring a range of benefits back into everyday life, from fellowship and improved health through to fitness and substantial wealth (as well as having some harmful consequences, with injuries being common).[28] The point, however, is that these consequences are not the 'end' of the game itself. The player does not kick the ball beyond the outstretched fingers of the goalkeeper, because it is good for their health. They do it because scoring a goal is the purpose of the game. Likewise, the person playing chess does not make the move Bxc6++ because it is good for improving concentration (which improves performance in the office and so boosts the monthly pay cheque). They do so because checkmate is the aim of the game. In other words, there are consequences to play but these consequences are secondary. The point of the game is in itself.

To put this in technical terms, play is *autotelic*. It has its own (*auto*) purpose (*telos*), enjoying a relative independence from the rest of life.[29] We sense something of this through the preposition 'at'. You win *at* sport. This – as Conner argues – is subtly different from winning *the* battle, *the* trophy or *the* match. You do not win the sport, you win *at* it. You do not therefore – in the same way as you do with trophies and spoils – possess the game. It retains sovereignty, so to speak, over the players. The only way to know that a player has won the game is by the rules. They alone measure success and failure. They are genuinely absolute. We do not possess anything. The game is free of us.[30]

With this in mind, we can begin to identify play as a radically contingent, self-contained and utterly absorbing, unnecessary-yet-meaningful activity. This echoes Huizinga's portrayal of play, which – as the theologian Robert K. Johnston notes – has become the most widely used analytic description of play today:[31]

> [Play is] a free activity standing quite consciously outside 'ordinary' life . . . but at the same time absorbing the player intensely and utterly. It is an activity connected with no material interest, and no profit can be gained from it. It proceeds within its own proper boundaries of time and space according to fixed rules and in an orderly manner.[32]

To put it otherwise, play *is* just play in itself.

The autotelic nature of play – we should note – does not devalue it. We do not have to spend time looking for a worthier reason. We should simply accept that play is what it is: it is radically unnecessary but internally meaningful. It is genuinely free from the serious business of life.[33]

III

But if this is how we are to understand play, what then of sport? What distinguishes sport – as a subspecies of play – from all other forms of play? Here the work of Allen Guttmann is of help. Guttmann divides play into two broad types, that which is *spontaneous* and that which is *regulated*.[34] Spontaneous play is impulsive and underdetermined, arising unexpectedly, voluntarily and unannounced. Such play is not premeditated. It is spur-of-the-moment and unplanned. A Nobel laureate might have some fun playing with words, making an off-the-cuff witty remark in a speech. Or a child might skim a stone across the surface of a lake.[35] These events give us an immediate sense of freedom, an opening up of possibilities beyond the norm. The freedom of the unexpected – breaking away from script – provides 'an ecstatic sense of pure possibility'.[36]

In contrast, regulated play is determined by its clear rules, which are freely embraced and become the means by which play is turned into *games*. A game is rule-bound play. Guttmann then argues that *games* – as a regulated form of play – can be further divided, this time along the line of competition. Some games – Guttmann notes, for example, 'leapfrog' – are not designed to produce a winner, while others, such as tennis, are. Games that do produce winners are known as *contests*, and within such contests a final distinction can be made. Some contests are settled on the basis of *physical prowess* (in that they involve a bodily attempt to overcome an unnecessary obstacle),[37] while others such as chess – though not devoid of a physical aspect – measure the players' *intellect*. Harnessing this fourfold distinction within play, Guttmann defines sport as a regulated, physical contest that serves its own ends. This is how sport is distinguished from other forms of play.[38]

There are other ways to distinguish between different forms of play.[39] Roger Caillois, for example, adopts a light-handed approach, purposively highlighting the overlapping and interconnected features of various forms of play.[40] He argues that play can centre on *mimicry*, the creating of illusions, imaginary universes and make-believe (though makes the point that all games – including sports – will have an element of mimicry in them). Or games can take the form of *ilinx*, a term he borrows from the Greek meaning 'whirlpool' and which he employs to designate games that seek to transform perception through some type of vertigo (such as the Whirling Dervishes or – more locally – motorsports, fairs and amusement parks). Alongside mimicry and ilinx, Caillois places *agôn*, a term which designates those forms of play that artificially create a competitive rivalry by establishing equality – a level playing field, so to speak – in order to measure a specific quality, such as speed, memory, strength and the like. Here, perhaps, we would place a sport such as football. For Caillois, however, we should not move too soon. Games also take the form of *alea*, which is a Latin word for dice, in which the player's success is determined solely by chance, their control shifting from the player to 'Lady Luck'. Though a competitive rivalry can exist, muscle and intelligence are rendered irrelevant, and unlike agôn – where work, practice, and training are rewarded – alea ignores such discipline. Instead, it involves a passive form of surrender to the judgement of the gods. Picture a game of roulette.

Under Caillois' fourfold classification, any act of play will combine these four ingredients to a greater or lesser extent. Each game will exhibit distinct proportions between skill and luck within an imaginary universe that transcends immediate perception to change experience. It is simply a question of degree rather than hard demarcation. Thus most games can be played alone or in teams, be competitive or reward achievement through varying degrees of physical effort, natural skill and irreducible luck. In other words, every sport will share a great deal in common with other games, though the balance between these various attributes will differ. What they all have in common, however, is their most basic characteristic: every form of play is a fundamentally unnecessary-yet-meaningful activity. This lies at the heart of any definition.[41]

But this is not our final definition of sport. Instead, we need to see these ideas as a number of analytic notes that complement our initial historical soundings. Freedom, non-necessity, meaning, order and rule-bound competition have now reverberated through the course of this chapter, along with physicality and relative independence. These analytic notes on sport sound out alongside the earlier historical threefold chord of popularity, opposition and instrumental use. The task now is to attempt to harmonize these various notes within a theological vision of the world in which we live. Our understanding of sport must be faithful to the gospel of Jesus Christ.

Notes

1 Others – perhaps George Orwell – might instead want to say that sport is a type of battle, a form of war ('minus the shooting'). This is a terrible mistake to make, misunderstanding both the nature of sport and the nature of war, as we will see in Chapter 9. For Orwell's critique of sport, see George Orwell, *The Sporting Spirit* (1945), available at: http://orwell.ru/library/articles/spirit/english/e_spirit.

2 'We *play* sport, we don't *work* sport.' Susan A. Jackson and Mihaly Csikszentmihalyi, *Flow in Sports*, Champaign, IL: Human Kinetics, 1999, p. 142.

3 'Animals play just like men.' Johan Huizinga, *Homo Ludens: A Study of the Play Element in Culture*, Boston, MA: Beacon Press, 1955, p. 1. Francis of Assisi – the great proponent of playful joy, a 'fool of Christ' – famously loved all the animals apart from ants, who he believed worked too much and did not know how to have fun.

4 Robert Johnston helpfully summarizes various understandings of the function of sport: the discharge of surplus energy (cf. Herbert Spencer, J. C. Friedrich von Schiller); recuperation from exhaustion (cf. G. T. W. Patrick, Moritz Lazarus); an instinct educator (cf. Karl Groos); a safety valve to vent emotions (cf. Aristotle); the creative modelling of possible situations to help handle future experience (cf. Erik Erikson); a means to resolve psychic conflict (cf. Freud). See Robert K. Johnston, *The Christian at Play*, Grand Rapids, MI: Eerdmans, 1997, p. 32.

5 'All these [explanations] . . . have one thing in common: they all start from the assumption that play must serve something which is *not* play, that it must have some kind of biological purpose . . . [And as] a rule they leave the primary quality of play, as such, virtually untouched. To each and every one of . . . [these] "explanations" it might well be objected: "so far so good, but what actually is the *fun* of playing?"' Huizinga, *Homo Ludens*, pp. 2–3.

6 Huizinga puts it in the negative: 'From the point of view of a world wholly determined by the operation of blind forces, play would be altogether superfluous.' Huizinga, *Homo Ludens*, pp. 3–4.

7 'The need for it is only urgent to the extent that the enjoyment of it makes it a need. Play can be deferred or suspended at any time. It is never imposed by physical necessity or moral duty. It is never a task.' Huizinga, *Homo Ludens*, p. 8.

8 'There is also no doubt that play must be defined as a free and voluntary activity, a source of joy and amusement. A game which one would be forced to play would at once cease being play. It would become constraint, drudgery from which one would strive to be freed. As an obligation or simply an order, it would lose one of its basic characteristics: the fact that the player devotes himself spontaneously to the game, of his free will and for his pleasure, each time completely free to choose retreat, silence, meditation, idle solitude, or creative activity.' Roger Caillois, *Man, Play and Games*, trans. Meyer Barash, Urbana and Chicago, IL: University of Illinois Press, 2001, p. 6. Of course, sometimes we only eat, drink or sleep because we want to. The point however is that it is hard *not* to want to at some stage. And even in extreme cases such as hunger strikes or anorexia – where, to an extent, someone chooses not to eat – someone can still be forced; that is the point.

9 'People work because they have to; they play because they want to.' Allen Guttmann, *Sports: The First Five Millennia*, Amherst and Boston, MA: University of Massachusetts Press, 2004, p. 1.

10 Guttmann, *Sports*, p. 2.

11 Steven Conner, *A Philosophy of Sport*, London: Reaktion Books, 2011, p. 20.

12 Walter J. Ong, 'Preface', in Hugo Rahner, *Man at Play*, New York: Herder and Herder, 1967, p. ix.

13 'There is a place for play: as needs dictate, the space for hopscotch, the board for checkers or chess, the stadium, the racetrack, the list, the ring, the stage, the arena, etc. Nothing that takes place outside this ideal frontier is relevant. To leave the enclosure by mistake, accident, or necessity, to send the ball out of bounds, may disqualify or entail a penalty.' Caillois, *Man, Play and Games*, p. 6.

14 Johnston, *The Christian at Play*, p. 34. See also, Shirl James Hoffman, *Good Game: Christianity and the Culture of Sports*, Waco, TX: Baylor University Press, 2010, p. 276.

15 Huizinga, *Homo Ludens*, p. 9. 'Many games do not imply rules. No fixed or rigid rules exist for playing with dolls, for playing soldiers, cops and robbers, horses, locomotives, and airplanes – games, in general, which presuppose free improvisation . . . [T]he sentiment of *as if* replaces and performs the same function as do rules. Rules create fictions. The one who plays chess, prisoner's base, polo, or baccarat, by the very fact of complying with their respective rules, is separated from real life where there is no activity that literally corresponds to any of these games. That is why chess, prisoner's base, polo, and baccarat are played *for real. As if* is not necessary.' Caillois, *Man, Play and Games*, p. 8. Caillois later makes the link between *illusion* and *in-lusio* ('to begin a game') to argue that play is to enter into an imaginary universe (p. 19).

16 'In every case, the game's domain is therefore a restricted, closed, protected universe: a pure space.' Caillois, *Man, Play and Games*, p. 7.

17 See Conner, *Philosophy of Sport*, pp. 146–83.

18 Conner, *Philosophy of Sport*, p. 146.

19 Conner, *Philosophy of Sport*, p. 14.

20 Caillois, *Man, Play and Games*, p. 10.

21 Conner, *Philosophy of Sport*, pp. 172–3.

22 Thanks to Nick Mercer for pointing out the connection between internal contingency and the word 'ludicrous'.

23 Conner, *Philosophy of Sport*, pp. 130–1.

24 This is soccer. To make the same point in an American format: 'Football is beautiful but meaningless; i.e., it makes no sense, pragmatically speaking. Certainly nothing could be more absurd than to hire a small army of godlike brutes, gifted with fantastic speed, strength, grace and coordination, to advance a leather ball down a gridiron.' Peter Heinegg, 'Philosophy of Football', *Christian Century* 91.43 (18 December 1974), p. 1198.

25 'Just asking for the purpose of a game makes a person a spoilsport.' Jürgen Moltmann, *Theology and Joy*, London: SCM Press, 1973, p. 31. 'The game is ruined by the nihilist who denounces the rules as absurd and conventional, who refuses to play because the game is meaningless. His arguments are irrefutable. The game has no other but an intrinsic meaning. That is why its rules are imperative and absolute, beyond discussion. There is no reason for their being as they are, rather than otherwise.' Caillois, *Man, Play and Games*, p. 7.

26 Huizinga, *Homo Ludens*, p. 8.

27 Though play can create a sense of achievement or fulfilment, a general consensus remains: 'A characteristic of play . . . is that it creates no wealth or goods, thus differing from work or art. At the end of the game, all can and must start over again at the same point. Nothing has been harvested or manufactured, no masterpiece has been created, no capital has accrued. Play is an occasion of pure waste: waste of time, energy, ingenuity, skill, and often of money . . .' Caillois, *Man, Play and Games*, p. 6.

28 See, for example, the correlation between sport and injury in Hoffman, *Good Game*, pp. 175–89.

29 Guttmann, *Sports*, p. 1.

30 Conner, *Philosophy of Sport*, p. 146.

31 Johnston, *The Christian at Play*, p. 33.

32 Huizinga, *Homo Ludens*, p. 13.

33 This insight is taken from the work of James Nuechterlein, who rightly concluded: 'a cigar, Freud noted, is sometimes just a cigar. Just so, and the Super Bowl is always just a football game. It does not make it less to refuse to make it more'. James Nuechterlein, 'The Wide World of Sports', *First Things* 49 (1995), pp. 8–9.

34 Guttmann, *Sports*, p. 1.

35 Guttmann, *Sports*, p. 1.

36 Guttmann, *Sports*, p. 1.

37 Conner, *Philosophy of Sport*, p. 15; cf. Bernard Suits. Conner nicely summarized, 'sports are games that tire you'.

38   As Guttmann puts it, a sport is an 'autotelic physical contest'. Guttmann, *Sports*, p. 3.

39   The task of definition is not simply the preserve of philosophical enquiry. Sport England – previously known as the Sports Council (and here leaning on the Council of Europe's earlier Sports Charter of 1993) – currently defines sport as: '[a] form of physical activity which, through casual or organized participation, aim[s] at expressing or improving physical fitness and mental well-being, forming social relationships or obtaining results in competition at all levels'. Something is a sport for the Sports Council when it has what it terms an 'Essential Purpose', which, on being spelt out, means: 'The purpose of the activity must be sporting and not a means to another purpose.' In short, sport must be *self-contained*. See http://www.sportengland.org/about_us/recognised_sports/how_we_recognise_sports.aspx.

40   Caillois, *Man, Play and Games*, pp. 14–36.

41   Caillois argues that play can be defined as an activity that is essentially:

1   *Free*: in which playing is not obligatory; if it were, it would at once lose its attractive and joyous quality as a diversion;

2   *Separate*: circumscribed within limits of space and time, defined and fixed in advance;

3   *Uncertain*: the course of which cannot be determined, nor the result attained beforehand, and some latitude for innovations being left to the player's initiative;

4   *Unproductive*: creating neither goods, nor wealth, nor new elements of any kind; and, except for the exchange of property among the players, ending in a situation identical to that prevailing at the beginning of the game;

5   *Governed by rules*: under conventions that suspend ordinary laws, and for the moment establish new legislation, which alone counts;

6   *Make-believe*: accompanied by a special awareness of a second reality or of a free unreality, as against real life.

In other words, we are free *to* play, play is free *from* outside purpose and it is free *in* outcome. Whichever way you look at it, play is free. Caillois, *Man, Play and Games*, pp. 9–10.

7

Towards a Christian Theology of Sport

To approach a Christian theology of sport, we need to dig deep. Our excavations need to take us into the heart of who God is and what he is up to. Any other approach will inevitably fall short. This is because we can understand sport only if we first appreciate who we really are; sport has everything to do with our most basic identity. That is why it is so unstoppably popular.

In this chapter, we therefore turn to the Church's core teachings about God and the act of creation. In so doing, we move into new territory. We will be dealing with some weighty concepts and some abstract ideas, now pursuing various leads that stem from the Church's confession that Jesus Christ is Lord. This means that we will be exploring how Christians understand God's own *godliness*, so to speak, as well as drawing out key implications from the Church's teachings about the way God made the world. These ideas will at once be quite simple yet at the same time bewilderingly complex. We should not be surprised at this. We are dealing with God *and* everything else. It is going to require some serious thinking.

Yet we must not shy away from the task. Only through knowledge of who we are in relation to God can we gather the necessary information to develop a Christian theology of sport. It is therefore time for us to engage directly with Christian belief.

II

Christians believe that God created everything.[1] This deceptively simple statement – straightforward in many respects – can be easily misunderstood. Without thinking too much about it, we can draw a straight line from the divine act of creation to our own creativity, mistakenly imagining that the act of creation is similar to what a person does when they invent a gadget or genetically modify a crop. However, these actions – inventive though they are – are better described as a formation or manipulation of reality. From a Christian perspective, they are certainly not creation. Only God creates. Put otherwise, *there is only one God*.

As God's action before anything else existed, the act of creation remains irreducibly mysterious.[2] Of course, there are better or worse ways to break the appropriate silence, and so Christians do use numerous models to depict what actually happened in the beginning. These various models draw from the relevant biblical imagery, especially that found in the Wisdom and Prophetic literature, as well as in the book of Genesis.[3] The overall witness of Scripture is clear: the one God creates a world that is *not God*.[4]

It is this simple insight that fuels the relentless opposition to idolatrous worship that we find in the Bible. Author after author battles furiously against the apostate practices of Israel, warning God's people that theirs is a jealous God who will brook no rival. Do not copy other nations, they cry. Do not worship the sun, moon or stars. These are simply ornaments that God has hung up in the sky to mark times and seasons. They are not God.[5] This message rings repeatedly. Anyone reading the Bible discovers that nature – in whatever form it takes – is not to be worshipped. Only God is. That is the first commandment.[6]

The Christian doctrine of creation simply unpacks the primary claim that there is only one God. But because there are no other gods, the Church also makes the claim that the one God created everything *out of nothing*. In adding this supplementary clause, Christians are peering back into the beginning of time through the witness of Jesus Christ, recognizing that the God of Israel who raised Jesus from the dead is the very God who would create life in a virgin's womb who is the very God who would summon everything into existence out of nothing. Therefore, Christians believe that there is a straight line back to the act of creation, but the line is not from our own inventive works. It is instead from Jesus Christ alone. We understand creation through him, the work of God.

Given this christological claim, the doctrine of creation functions – right from the outset – as an axiom of theological speech for Christians. In fact, it was so obvious that God created everything out of nothing that it immediately became a part of theological debate that went without saying, and so it was rarely said and seldom written down. As a result, there is no winding road – as there is with the doctrines of God and Jesus Christ – to the Council of Wherever.[7] Instead, all we find in the early Church are ridiculing polemics, which are often targeted at Gnostic sects that were seeking to place God and creation in one multi-storeyed universe, a singularly slippery slope from spirit down to matter. As Irenaeus made clear, these sects were wrong for a whole host of reasons.[8] For Christians, however, the true logic was obvious: because creation is not divine, it must be made out of nothing, because there was nothing in the beginning except God.

With the foundational premise obvious to the Church, it was the implications that needed to be teased out. The trail ran in a number of directions. First, if in eternity there is only God, then God's hand – at the point of creation – cannot have been forced in any way, because there was nothing around to force it. In other words, because there is only one God, nothing determined his action other than himself (not even 'nothing'). This means that Christians believe that God's act of creation was radically *free*. God cannot be pushed around.[9]

Some Christians are tempted to think there was a subtle, indirect compulsion behind the act of creation, some irresistible itch that God had to scratch. They might imagine

that 'nothing' – though not a thing – is a kind of *need*, a deficiency if you like. It might denote an emptiness, an absence,
a hollowness in God, perhaps even a type of loneliness.
Perhaps God was all by himself in eternity, somewhat bored
with nothing to do? Maybe he had to create to have some
company? Maybe he created because he needed to love?

The Church has always rejected such claims.[10] It instead con-
fesses that there is neither a need nor a deficiency in God which
creation is designed to fix. This is because God is complete in
himself *eternally*.[11]

The perfect fullness of God is hard to express, but it centres
on the belief that the creator God – the one Christians come to
know in Jesus Christ – *is* the eternal communion of three persons-
in-relation, Father, Son and Holy Spirit. These Three give and
receive existence from and to each other in the dynamic event
of interdependent reciprocity. They exist into and out of each
other, generating and embracing eternal being in the unsurpass-
able procession and begetting of eternal life in communion. In
other words, the Christian God is one simultaneous, harmonious
and sustaining act by which the Father, Son and Spirit are who
they are in the singular event of being interrelated in a dynamic
movement of self-emptying and self-giving, the intense singular-
ity of perfect communion as gift. Put more simply: God *is* love.[12]

And, just so, as love, God does not need to create anything,
because he keeps his own company, so to speak.[13] An important implication springs immediately from this claim. Because
the triune God is complete in himself, he creates freely, and this
means that the 'thing' God creates also has an integrity.[14] This
is true because – in saying that the Father, Son and Spirit created the world out of nothing – the Church had found a way of
saying that God did not make the world out of God. In effect,
out of nothing implies that creation is not a broken-off piece
of God-stuff that God falsely rebrands as a 'creature'. Nor is
the world made out of some co-eternal 'matter' that God finds
lying around beside himself and pretends is not divine.[15] Instead,
out of nothing implies that God freely summons a world into
existence and that this world is *really* creaturely.[16]

The integrity of creation means that no matter how hard we scrape away at appearances, no matter how deep we dig into facts, no matter how far we travel through the universe, we will never get to a non-creaturely bit of it; creation is creation from top to bottom.[17] That said, there are things that we will want to say about Jesus Christ here, not least the simultaneous fullness of his divinity and humanity, but we want to say these things precisely because in him – and only in him – divinity and creation perfectly coincide. He *is* the God-man, which is why the Church stands in awe of him. But the same does not apply to anyone or anything else. Instead, Christians believe there is a stark difference between God and the world he has made, and this difference is not quantitative; it is *qualitative*.

The qualitative difference between God and the world means that God is not simply older than us, cleverer than us, stronger than us or more beautiful than us. The Church instead says that the difference between God and creation is much greater than that; it is qualitative, and the qualitative difference is infinite – hence the irreducible mystery of the incarnation. *God* became man.[18]

With this qualitative difference in mind, the Church can say that the created order has its own integral reality which is distinct from God's. Of course, it *is* related to God (the Creator) and utterly depends on God (the Sustainer), but creation is *not* God. We could even venture to say that that creation is *secular* in being, a term that rightly indicates creation's relative self-standing from God, in that God gives it space to be.

The secularizing function of the Christian doctrine of creation has a number of important implications. Many scholars now recognize that it enables the emergence of modern science, for example, a fact that runs contrary to the pernicious myth that all forms of scientific belief are incompatible with the Christian faith. Once the Church proclaims the integrity of creation, people are freed to explore it with their eyes open, because the truth of the world does not reside in some eternal blueprint – such as the Platonic Forms – that is only accessible through abstract reasoning. Its truth is instead contingent and so our posture towards it changes.[19] Simply put, you do not shoot rockets at the moon if you think it is a goddess.[20]

But our trail leads away from the integrity of creation in a different – but related – direction.[21] If the Christian account is true, then all creatures – being neither God nor needed by God – are not that 'serious', as Rowan Williams puts it.[22] Instead creatures are essentially groundless, with no 'density and solidity' other than that which they receive as the pure gift of being suspended on 'the divine communication over an unfathomable abyss'.[23] To be created out of nothing therefore means that there is no landscape outside of God's summoning speech. It renders us irreducibly – and continuously – *graced*. We are held in existence only by the divine will that we *be*. There is no other support, only nothingness.

With this in mind, we can see that to be created is to be continuously invited into existence. But it is never to possess that existence by right. Of course, this leaves us with an inescapable lightness of being, something that many people find unbearable. We yearn instead for something – anything! – upon which we might raise a flag of independence and from which we can begin to barter with God as (almost) equals. This move is the essence of the Fall. It is to ascribe to ourselves a 'nature' that is not graced. It is to take ourselves too seriously. But the good news is that there is no territory that is not grace. There is no lasting substance that we can rebrand as *nature* and claim as our own possession. Instead, we are created freely out of nothing, and remain irreducibly and unavoidably at the mercy of God. That is what creation must mean to the Christian. And this is a delight. It means we do not have to carry the weight of eternity around on our shoulders. Everything was fine without us.[24]

All of this can be easily misunderstood. The non-serious nature of creation can be conceived as a form of nihilism, an inescapable meaninglessness that plunges us headlong down into despair. But make no mistake. The Church has never said there is no meaning to life. Creation may not be serious, but it is not meaningless. Instead, the Church believes that we are created freely *out* of nothing and *for* something.[25]

Two things need to be said about this claim. First, the Church believes that in eternity – at the heart of the joyful converse of the triune life – the Three decided to share their life with a fourth. God, though completely perfect in himself, freely elected to open up his life, making room for the creature to share the endless life of loving communion. The creature is therefore invited to join with him – a counterpoint to the triune harmony – in indescribably glorious fellowship with the Son in union with the Spirit before the Father. Precisely thus, our non-necessity is no reason for despair. Though we have been summoned from nothing, we have been summoned by Love *for* love. This is the purpose of the creature.[26]

But a second thing needs to be said. The Church believes that the purpose of the creature is in Jesus Christ. Everything was created in him, through him and for him, and holds together in him.[27] In other words, when God summoned the world into existence, he said 'Jesus', the Son and the Spirit patiently establishing and perfecting a time, place and people for the coming incarnation of the Son of God. Everything – from galaxies, moons, mountains and lakes – was swept up in this dynamic movement towards communion in Christ and can only find its meaning in him. Our end is in Christ – which is again to say creation has meaning and its meaning is love.[28]

But what is important for us to recognize is that this is a *freely* expressed purpose. There was no blueprint that God had to adhere to as he brought this about in Christ. There was no architectural plan he was contracted to follow, no rational blueprint he was forced to meet. Instead, he acted freely. This means that things could really be different from how they now are. *That* God elected to make sun, moon and stars, with mountains and trees, and talking featherless bipeds called human beings, *is* somewhat arbitrary. Viewed from the outside – if that was possible – it would make just as much sense for human beings to have thirteen legs, six necks and a dozen heads. It was God's free decision that it be otherwise.

This is to say that God's free decision to create took concrete form. Creation is lovingly purposed in Jesus Christ. In effect,

God decides to be the generous God who opens up his life in communion with the creature, and this decision is Jesus. As a result – even though we know things *could* be different – it now makes complete sense that human beings have only two arms and two legs because of who Jesus is. Creation is ordered to him and ruled by him. Jesus is the meaning of life.

To be created is therefore to be part of the unnecessary but meaningful movement from nothingness towards love in Jesus Christ. Or, from the other direction, the Creator is *the one who loves us in the freedom of Jesus.*[29] God has not created us as part of some extrinsic economy between rival gods. God did not create us because he had to prove himself to someone who was judging his work. God did not create us for any purpose beyond or outside the event of Jesus Christ. The reason for creation is therefore intrinsic to the creature, because it *is* Jesus Christ and he is fully human. This is what the Church believes.

III

Much more will need to be said about all this, not least of the way in which – completely absurdly – the creature rejects Love, preferring instead to curve in on itself, seeking the nothingness from which it was summoned rather than the life to which it is called. Destroying our meaning on a cross outside Jerusalem, we tried to un-create ourselves.[30] But, with this tragic complexity noted, our exploration of the doctrine of creation allows us to draw out two key points. These two points combine to teach us that creation is essentially *unnecessary yet meaningful.*

Hopefully, we can see that this theological conclusion maps neatly onto the working definition of play that was developed in the previous chapter. There we concluded that play is an unnecessary but meaningful activity. As a result, we can now join up these two dots. The Christian doctrine of creation allows us to understand that our being – our *is*-ness, so to speak – is best described as the unnecessary-yet-meaningful reality of being freely loved into existence in Jesus Christ. This would suggest that when we play – unnecessary but meaningfully – we are living out our deepest identity as unnecessary but meaningful creatures. Simply put, we reverberate with ourselves. We chime with our being. This is the key insight we must take into the next chapter.

Notes

1 One of the finest studies of the Christian doctrine of creation remains Colin E. Gunton, *The Triune Creator: A Historical and Systematic Study*, Grand Rapids, MI: Eerdmans, 1998. Readers seeking further instruction in these matters are directed there. For any reader familiar with his work, my debt to Gunton's thinking will be evident throughout.

2 Of course, we bump up against the problem of language straight away. It is difficult to speak of anything *before* creation as time is part of creation. Yet, the point remains: in speaking of creation, we speak of something before everything else and so not comparable to anything else.

3 For example: Job 38.1–42.6; Proverbs 8.22–31; Psalms 104 and 74.12–17.

4 'The first proposition: that God creates means that there is other reality than God *and that it is really other than he.*' Robert Jenson, Systematic Theology, vol. 2, *The Works of God*, New York and Oxford: Oxford University Press, 1999, p. 5, emphasis added.

5 See discussion in Gunton, *Triune Creator*, pp. 17–18.

6 Stephen R. Holmes makes the case that Scripture is primarily about *monaltry* (worshipping one God) as it is about *monotheism* (there being one God). See Stephen R. Holmes, *The Holy Trinity: Understanding God's Life*, Milton Keynes: Paternoster, 2012, pp. 45–6.

7 'The doctrine of creation out of nothing was accepted, it seems, almost immediately and unanimously.' David A. S. Fergusson, *The Cosmos and the Creator: An Introduction to the Theology of Creation*, London: SPCK, 1998, p. 31. 'The adoption of the view that the world was created out of nothing was almost universal in Christian circles very quickly.' Frances Young, '"Creatio Ex Nihilo": A Context for the Emergence of the Christian Doctrine of Creation', *Scottish Journal of Theology*, vol. 44 (1991), p. 150. Steven Toulmin – in his brilliant review of Western modernity – makes the case that world-views *always* rest on hidden scaffolds, the parts of our thinking that go without saying and are therefore rarely said. For the Church, the doctrine of creation is one such scaffold. Stephen Toulmin, *Cosmopolis: The Hidden Agenda of Modernity*, Chicago, IL: University of Chicago Press, 1992. Eventually, with the resurgence of Aristotelian teaching under the influence of Islam, the Church did spell things out. In the Confession of Faith at the Fourth Lateran Council in 1215, it states: 'We firmly believe and simply confess that there is only one true God . . . creator of all things invisible and visible, spiritual and corporeal; who by his almighty power at the beginning of time

created from nothing both spiritual and corporeal creatures, that is to say angelic and earthly, and then created human beings composed as it were of both spirit and body in common.' And Session 11 of the Council of Florence (1442) states: 'Most firmly it believes, professes and preaches that the one true God, Father, Son and Holy Spirit, is the creator of all things that are, visible and invisible, who, when he willed it, made from his own goodness all creatures, both spiritual and corporeal, good indeed, because they are made by the supreme good, but mutable because they are made from nothing.'

8 See Irenaeus, *Against Heresies*.

9 Cf. Henry Chadwick on impassibility.

10 See, for one example, the *Catechism of the Catholic Church*: 'We believe that God needs no preexistent thing or any help in order to create, nor is creation any sort of necessary emanation from the divine substance. God creates freely "out of nothing".' *Catechism of the Catholic Church*, § 296.

11 See this logic at work, for example, in Karl Barth, *Dogmatics in Outline*, London: SCM Press, 1949, pp. 35–64.

12 For a gentle introduction to the Christian doctrine of God, see Tim Chester, *Delighting in the Trinity*, Grand Rapids, MI and Oxford: Monarch Books, 2005, and Michael Reeves, *The Good God: Enjoying Father, Son and Spirit*, Milton Keynes: Paternoster, 2012. For a wonderful analysis of the God of the gospel, see Robert W. Jenson, *The Triune Identity: God According to the Gospel*, Eugene, OR: Wipf and Stock, 2002. In my opinion, Jenson's book remains one of the best books available on the Christian doctrine of God.

13 Conner concludes that we are 'the unnecessary animal', but can give no reason for this non-necessity. In fact he seems to see each individual person as unnecessary particulars of the necessity which is humanity. Our account is very different. Conner, *A Philosophy of Sport*, pp. 25–6.

14 This is one of the main themes of Gunton, *The Triune Creator*. See, for example: '[T]here are two requirements for a satisfactory construal of the relation of God and the world: adequate conceptions of the continuing relatedness of the world to God and of that world's due reality – we might say due autonomy, better expressed as that is in the German *Selbständigkeit* – in its relation to God' (p. 101).

15 If he did, monotheism would be a lie.

16 'In a trinitarian understanding, because God has otherness – personal freedom and "space" – within the dynamics of his being, he is able to grant to the world space to be itself.' Colin E. Gunton, *The Promise of Trinitarian Theology*, 2nd edn, London and New York: T & T Clark, 2003, p. 202.

17 '[T]he only divinity is the Creator God, while creatures are creatures all the way down.' Robert Jenson, *On Thinking the Human: Resolutions of Difficult Notions*, Grand Rapids, MI and Cambridge: Eerdmans, 2003, p. 25.

18 Put otherwise: '[T]he archangel may look vastly superior to the worm from where we stand, but in the light of divine existence they are so close in being as to be indistinguishable.' Holmes, *The Holy Trinity*, p. 96.

19 The most important essay on this subject remains Michael Foster, 'The Christian Doctrine of Creation and the Rise of Modern Science', *Mind* 43 (1934), pp. 446–68.

20 Robert W. Jenson, *Systematic Theology*, vol. 2, *The Works of God*, Oxford: Oxford University Press, 1999, p. 115.

21 In conversation, Graham Tomlin has echoed Jenson's point about the doctrine of creation and the emergence of science in relation to one particular sport: the reason we now climb mountains is precisely because we no longer believe that the gods live at their summits. Mountaineering is an indirect result of the Christian doctrine of creation.

22 Rowan Williams, *Not Being Serious: Thomas Merton and Karl Barth* (2008), available at http://rowanwilliams.archbishopofcanterbury.org/articles. php/1205/not-being-serious-thomas-merton-and-karl-barth.

23 Williams, *Not Being Serious*.

24 In an attempt to avoid the 'the old hemi-demi-semi-Pelagian temptation', Robert Jenson makes the point that a longstanding distinction between natural and supernatural must be questioned. Jenson's solution is to recognize that 'nature and grace are aspects of one conversation conducted by God with us'. More biblically framed, '"Let there be . . ." and "Christ is risen" are but two utterances of God within one dramatically coherent discourse. A creature who exists by hearing the first is indeed open to the second, in a straightforward way that requires no dithering about "aptitudes".' 'We are indeed prepared in our very nature for the deifying address of God, because we have a nature only in that we have already been caught up by the dialogue in which this concluding address occurs.' Jenson, *Systematic Theology*, vol. 2, pp. 66–8.

25 '"It's all *for nothing* anyway," says the nihilist and falls into despair. "It's really all *for nothing*," says the believer, rejoicing in the grace which he can have for nothing and hoping for a new world in which all is available and may be had *for nothing*.' Moltmann, *Theology and Joy*, p. 54.

26 Creation, as Rowan Williams concludes, exists because, 'God loves and it *is* for no other reason.' Williams, *Not Being Serious*.

27 Cf. Colossians 1.

28 This approach will strike many minds as counter-intuitive. It rests on the belief that creation needs to be understood as a movement towards Christ (the Son and the Spirit moving towards the point of incarnation from the very beginning). There is a long tradition in the Church that wants to keep creation and redemption closely connected, refusing to see incarnation as an afterthought (a Plan B), but instead seeing Jesus Christ as the original plan (even if the Fall transforms the projected throne of the Son into a gallows). God's decision to create was his commitment to be Jesus Christ. John Duns Scotus (1266–1308) is a key authority in the debate, making the case that there would have been an incarnation without a Fall. For a short imaginative way to get to grips with the issue of creation being shaped to Jesus (rather than vice versa), see Robert W. Jenson, 'Christ as Culture 2: Christ as Art', *International Journal of Systematic Theology* 6.1 (2004), pp. 69–76.

29 This twofold insight into God's life drives the entire theology of Karl Barth. Barth is a very important inspiration in the theology attempted here. For a brief account of how he sees the non-serious nature of play, see the collected writings of Barth on his beloved Mozart. Karl Barth, *Wolfgang Amadeus Mozart*, Eugene, OR: Wipf and Stock, 2003.

30 On our reading, sin is taking ourselves too seriously. (G. K. Chesterton made the basic point, 'Angels can fly because they take themselves lightly; devils

fall because of their gravity.') Therefore, though we must say that the crucifixion is serious (we killed God!), the resurrection can be understood as God's refusal to take our false seriousness *seriously*. In so doing, a second glorious movement of grace begins, the fallen creature is invited into life with God. That is love. Here, in this account of sin, we differ from Steven Conner, who suggests that sin is frivolous: 'It is not just that sport was sinful because it was pointless: sin and evil were themselves sportive because of their essential frivolity, their lack of seriousness.' Steven Conner, *A Philosophy of Sport*, London: Reaktion Books, 2011, p. 22.

8

The Liturgical Celebration of Contingency: A Brief Theology of Sport

Up to this point, the constructive argument has proved relatively simple. It involves the joining together of two conceptual dots. If play and creation are both fundamentally unnecessary-but-meaningful realities, we can say that creatures at play are expressing their deepest identity as the ones freely loved into existence by God. The task now is to develop a theology of sport on the basis of this simple proposal.

We press on, however, knowing that things in the past have not been as straightforward as our thesis suggests. In the first part of the book, we went to some length in identifying ways in which the Church has engaged with sport. These earlier case studies showed that the Church – overall – appears to be unsure how to handle sport, with its characteristic approach fluctuating from outright opposition to unashamed attempts to harness sport to its own agenda. Neither approach has enjoyed much success. It seems that sport can be neither fully prohibited nor fully controlled. Irreducibly free, it knows no master.

Two immediate observations can be made on the back of this. First, the theological proposal puts us in a much better position to understand why sport has remained so popular despite regular opposition from the Church. If our proposal is true, then it will mean that people will always play sport, because people will always be playful. Given this most basic fact, the Church should be celebrating sport rather than opposing it.

Of course, there are many things which are popular that the Church will never celebrate. To take an obvious example: drunken sexual immorality is unlikely to be celebrated despite its broad fan base. But immoral behaviour, such as sex outside marriage, is a corrupted form of human living; it is not true to who we really are. But on our reckoning, sport is quite different. It expresses the heart of our identity. It should therefore be valued – though, as we shall see, this is not to claim it is uncorrupted.

Second, the proposal puts us in a much better position to judge whether the Church should be harnessing sport to its own agenda. This is because – as we saw in our earlier analysis – both sport and creation are radically free in having their own internal ends and goals. Because they are free in this way, we can see straight away that it will be a mistake to set sport in service to an outside agenda, be that ecclesial or secular. Many people instinctively sense this. When sport serves the corporate interests of big business and profit, for example, supporters feel uneasy, intuitively recognizing that money is corrupting the game through financial doping, the un-levelling of the playing field and the pollution of motives. We also sense something is wrong when sport is set to serve political agendas, be they right wing, left wing or straight down the middle. When the Nazis tried to connect the Olympics to their fascist ideology, or when scientists manipulated performance to prove the superiority of Soviet communism, sport was being corrupted by serving something other than sport. Our analysis has now shown why. The incorporation of external agendas into sport pollutes sport, because sport is radically autotelic. It should therefore be left alone.[1]

An important judgement can be made in light of this claim. Christians have been misguided – and continue to be misguided – when they attempt to harness sport to their own agenda. Though we will be able to think of many fine reasons why Christians *should* attempt to connect sport to their missional programmes – not least evangelism – these are not *sporting* reasons. This means that Christians will inevitably be corrupting the sport in question when they attempt to harness it. Given the eternal stakes involved, we may judge that the end justifies the means. But, if we do that, we should be clear what we are doing. With ulterior motives, Christians will – quite literally – be acting as spoilsports. The Church will be ruining the game by being overly serious.[2]

With this judgement made, we should recognize that it is very difficult to avoid the trap. It is far too tempting – and far too easy – to set play in service to an outside interest, be that biological, educational, political or ecclesial.[3] The work of the philosopher Sam Keen, for example, is a case in point. Keen's writings can be read as a true celebration of play, but in fact Keen is setting play to serve a therapeutic agenda.[4] For Keen, all forms of play are liberating counterpoints to the widespread 'dis-ease' of society, providing people with a means of escaping the alienating and sterile environment of modern life and its attempt to manipulate and control reality. Keen thinks that people – through play – can be freed from this social 'dis-grace', becoming psychologically healthy individuals who are at ease in a spontaneous present where they move playfully through life unencumbered by the delusions of control and manipulation. For Keen, therefore, play is essentially therapeutic in that it improves psychological health. This is why we should play. The reason is outside the game.

The theologian Jürgen Moltmann takes a different approach, though again he gives play a purpose outside itself.[5] For Moltmann, modern life is warped and twisted, with ordinary people alienated from reality through the unjust social structures that privilege a powerful elite. Fuelled instead by his hopeful vision of the Kingdom, Moltmann describes play as the gift of an eschatological reality in which the player joyfully moves in step with God as his Kingdom-life bursts into the present, momentarily shattering the yokes of slavery and liberating the person to experience transformed life. For Moltmann, therefore, play is a revolutionary act that liberates people into the freedom of the future. This is why we should play. Again the purpose is outside the game. It is political.

Robert K. Johnston rightly criticizes both Keen and Moltmann for giving play a purpose beyond itself.[6] Yet, almost without noticing, Johnston himself falls into the instrumentalist trap. He first recognizes what is at stake here, arguing that play 'must be entered into without outside purpose . . . [and] be connected with [no] material interest or ulterior motive'.[7] But having established this vital point, Johnston recognizes that play has a number of outside consequences, one of which – he argues – is a 'presentiment of the sacred'.[8]

In order to preserve his original definition, Johnston argues that play holds 'in tension a variety of polarities', an insight that allows him to highlight the playful tension between the real and the artificial, the individual and the communal, as well as that between spontaneity and design.[9] Having sketched these various tensions, Johnston introduces the novel idea of a 'non-instrumentality which is nevertheless productive', an idea which sets him off along a trajectory in which he argues that play is a form of worship, the liberator of a person's spirit. In short, it allows the person to move 'outward towards the sacred'.[10]

For Johnston, therefore, play is 'the avenue through which God communes with us', a means by which we encounter God. This, as Johnston recognizes, gives play 'an external value that reaches far beyond the boundary of the play world'.[11] Johnston therefore tries to step back from the position, underlining the freedom of God and arguing that a person cannot be certain they will move towards God in their play. This means – in Johnston's mind – that play (sometimes) does not serve an outside purpose. But the slope proves too slippery. Johnston is soon transforming the joy of play into 'the Joy of God', with play effectively becoming a servant of revelation. Like Keen and Moltmann before him, Johnston finds the reason to play outside of play. It is to enable us to meet with God. That is its purpose.[12]

Johnston is not alone in this. The Roman Catholic theologian Hugo Rahner makes a similar move. Like us, he first argues that play and creation are inextricably linked, with God's creative activity being understood as the 'playing of God'.[13]

Rahner tracks this motif through a wide range of literature. He finds it in pre-Socratic philosophers such as Heraclitus, as well as in ancient myths that 'oscillate between world–creation and world–play, between king and child . . . that tell of an infant God'.[14] In analysing these various accounts, Rahner concludes that the act of creation needs to be understood as a joyful, spontaneous liberty, springing forth from the hand of a child.[15] With this child-centred vision in mind, Rahner condenses his constructive argument into a succinct summary: 'Since God is a God who plays, man too must be a creature that plays: a *Homo ludens*.'[16]

Influenced by his reading of Plato, Rahner argues that play is a participation in the divine, a way in which our 'spirits return home to God'.[17] Play 'arises from the longing for the vision of the divine', serving as 'a secret preparatory exercise for the object of [the trapped spirit's] longing'.[18] As with Johnston, play has become an activity that brings the participant into the divine presence, a means of lively fellowship with God, which is otherwise known as worship.[19]

Rahner is not the first to confuse play with worship, and neither will he be the last. In fact, it is a very easy mistake to make, not least because of the family resemblance between the two. As we saw in the first part of the book, ancient cultures invariably saw sport as an aspect of religion, with sport functioning as a ritual retelling of the story of the gods and a means for petitionary intercession. History – it seems – would suggest that Rahner is on to something. Perhaps sport needs to be understood as a form of worship?

But history teaches us to tread carefully here. We have seen that the Church – with one or two exceptions – has worked hard to distinguish its worship from sport. Someone like the Dean of Auxerre did try to incorporate a ball game into the Easter liturgy back in the twelfth century, but his attempt is odd, because he was trying to do something that is so unusual for the Church.[20] In fact, *that* we do not instinctively see sport as a form of worship today – as most cultures in history have – is testimony to the Church's success in de-coupling the two.

For the Church, worship is worship and sport is sport; the two should not be confused.[21] Therefore, we must be careful in following the likes of Rahner and Johnston.

But if the Church teaches us that sport is not worship, how else can we understand it? To answer this question, we first recognize that there is a strong family resemblance between sport and worship.[22] This is especially clear with liturgical worship. Liturgy is an ordered physical activity in which a people – through rule-governed choreographed performance – cultivate a positive relationship with God.[23] Through their ordered singing, listening, responding, gesturing, praying and speaking, the people publicly symbolize *and* actualize the story of God-with-his-people. This liturgical action takes many forms, be that a Eucharist, a baptism, a traditional marriage service or innovative funeral. But whatever form it takes, an act of liturgy enables the Christian to celebrate who God is in the event of genuinely engaging with God through real-time, rule-governed symbolic instruments.[24]

In Christianity, therefore, liturgy is an ordered, determined prescribed rite of embodied worship, which becomes – through God's involvement in it – a genuine celebration of life-with-God. Just like play, this action does not create anything or achieve anything; there are no heavenly air miles awarded, so to speak. Instead, it is an activity with its own inner logic, its own intrinsic value; its own proper end: the free enjoyment of God with God.[25]

The connection we must make is hopefully clear. If, in light of the doctrine of creation, we can say that the creature enjoys a genuine existence on a trajectory out of nothing towards God, then we can say that sport is the liturgy – the irreducibly embodied dramatic communal actualization – of this most basic identity. When we play sport, we are celebrating our freely determined form as these particular creatures through a freely determined rule-governed unnecessary-but-meaningful activity. Through this radically contingent activity, we reverberate with ourselves in the integrity of our freedom. It is an event in which the creature, *as* itself, celebrates itself. In short, sport is a liturgy of our contingency.

This way of conceptualizing sport preserves its autotelic nature. When we go to a sporting event – be that to play or spectate, live or through media – it is not to make us healthier, wealthier, happier or anything like that. Nor does it take us beyond the event into communion with God. Instead, we are simply facing inwards and bouncing up against ourselves. This makes it a radically self-contained event, because it terminates on us – here and now – as we *are*. It is graced creatures living out grace. We chime with our own being.[26]

Therefore, the Church has been right. Sport is not worship. Worship is the liturgical celebration of who God is with us. Sport is the liturgical celebration of who we are by ourselves.[27]

This therefore raises the interesting question of whether *God* makes a distinction between worship and sport. Here we step into deep waters, raising a possibility that is almost beyond imagining. To get to that point, we must first question an aspect of our proposal: *can we really say that sport is for nothing other than sport?* This question needs to be asked, because Christians have always understood the whole of creation to be for the glory of God. The sun, moon and stars, the mountains, trees and animals, all in their own way are singing the praises of God. This means we must say that these things – at some level – are not for nothing. They are instead for the glory of God. Given that sport is part of the created order, surely it must also be for the glory of God? If so, it is not entirely for itself.

The way to approach an answer to this question is to clear up a possible misunderstanding. To say that creation is for nothing is not to deny that it is to the glory of God. Instead, it is to make the point that there is no ulterior motive beyond the event of creation. Creation was not the result of a divine bet or a dare, thereby set to serve an outside agenda in which God wins a reward or establishes his reputation. Instead, the act of creation is its own end: it *is* life-with-God-in-Jesus Christ. There is nothing beyond this. Creation is for creation's sake.

With this point clarified, we can recognize that God, in the act of creation, creates something that is *not* God. This means there is now a reality – upheld by God in Jesus Christ – which is genuinely other than God. In loving it, God the Father gives space to this reality, enabling it, through the Son and Spirit, to be held in existence close-yet-at-a-distance. This generous giving of space-in-relation – in which creation is neither God nor nothing – establishes an irreducible point of otherness which God in his grace allows. The very fabric of the creature – our ontological reality, so to speak – is genuinely given to us, held in existence by God as *other*. Simply put, there *is* something (which is not nothing) to which God relates as God.[28]

Now, in worship, God in his freedom is committed to being present to his people in this reality. He therefore steps forward, so to speak, to inhabit the liturgical action, becoming truly present with the creature in communion in Jesus Christ. In sport, however, the opposite is the case. God instead steps back, evacuating the space created by the liturgical action, enabling the creature to be somehow at a distance in its own integrity. In effect, in worship, God transcends the difference. In sport, God establishes the difference. He is in one. He is out of the other.[29]

On this reading, the ontological fabric of the creature is precisely the eventful space in which sport happens. A sporting event is a liturgy of the deserted point of irreducible otherness between ourselves, God and nothing, and – if this is the case – sport is to be understood as a haltering, fluttering, momentary event in which the creature is in and of itself on a trajectory out of nothing towards God. In sport, we are miraculously being ourselves, facing inwards into our space which is neither God nor nothing.

Of course, God creates us, sustains us and preserves the creation at all times, but sport is the miraculous liturgy of momentary distance in which he steps back, uninvolved, refusing to influence the outcome of a game in any way whatsoever. God instead enjoys watching us being ourselves as we pivot freely between himself and nothingness.[30] To put it otherwise, sport is only to the glory of God because it is for no reason other than itself. He allows this balletic self-standing. That is his generosity. That is his glory. And that is precisely what is so amazing about sport. It is not for God. It *is* simply the graceful creature.

We can therefore make a helpful distinction here between sport and the rest of our life. To understand this distinction, we first need to return to the question of worship. Earlier, I argued that worship – like play – has no extrinsic purpose; it serves no wider economy: it is an end in itself. But being for nothing, in this sense, does not lessen the value of our worship. The converse is in fact the case. Worship serves nothing. Instead everything serves worship.

To put it otherwise, worship is so valuable that it is the single determining purpose of everything else we do. All life is for the glory of God (see Eph. 1.11–12). This means that when we worship freely and joyfully, we are in harmony with our divinely appointed purpose to live with God. This is transparent in times of corporate thanksgiving, where we sing the praises of our Maker. But it is also lived out in our day-to-day work, our arts and our crafts, our science and our technology. The working creature – through the Son and Spirit – is here offering creation back to the Father with thanksgiving. And a life defined by worship is the creaturely voice – a fourth voice, so to speak – sounding as the counterpoint to the triune harmony. In effect, worship defines all that we do. It is our end. We are the 'praying animal', the priests of creation.[31]

But on this account, worship does not quite define everything. Sport is understood to be the only thing that is *not* worship. Or, to make the point the other way around: everything we do in our life serves our worship, *except* our sport. Sport is only for sport. It is the one thing that is not directed to the glory of God. That is what sets it apart.

Notes

1 Hitler believed that Aryans were the 'Master Race' and that this should translate into sporting success. He was therefore disappointed by the success of non-Aryans at the 1936 Olympics and so concluded that primitive people had an advantage given their 'wilder' ancestors; they should therefore be banned from civilized games. The Soviet approach was multifarious, looking to harness sport as part of a wider programme of social engineering. Sport helped build the nation, integrate a disparate population and keep them healthy, as well as help motivate large standing armies and a disaffected population, not least in drawing them away from religion. But all the evidence suggests that Soviet sports were riddled with doping programmes in which drug-taking was organized, systematic and politically motivated. For a discussion on Nazis in sport, see Albert Speer, *Inside the Third Reich*, New York: Simon & Schuster, 1997. See discussion at: http://sites.duke.edu/wcwp/research-projects/football-and-politics-in-europe-1930s-1950s/hitler-and-nazi-philosophy/#fn-1061-5. For communist approaches to sport, see James Riordan, 'The Impact of Communism on Sport', *Historical Social Research* 32.1 (2007), pp. 110–15. For evidence of drug use, see James Riordan, 'Soviet-style Sport in Eastern Europe: The End of an Era', in Lincoln Allison (ed.), *The Changing Politics of Sport*, Manchester: Manchester University Press, 1993, pp. 49–51. Even when sports are boycotted for good reasons, such as under Apartheid in South Africa, many inside and outside sport – often for the wrong reasons – want to keep sport free from politics. The stand-alone nature of sport is also in evidence when governing bodies are allowed to exercise jurisdiction over events, even when incidents would constitute criminal offences off the pitch. The police rarely extend their deference to the supporters, however.

2 This is not to rule out ad hoc witnessing by Christians in sport. It is instead to caution against programmes that seek to use sport strategically to this end. For further comments on this, see the discussion in the next chapter.

3 Huizinga warns that play all too quickly is set to serve something beyond itself, a 'quasi-rationalistic element irresistibly creep[ing] in'. Johan Huizinga, *Homo Ludens: A Study of the Play Element in Culture*, Boston, MA: Beacon Press, 1955, p. 17.

4 Robert K. Johnston, *The Christian at Play*, Grand Rapids, MI: Eerdmans, 1997, pp. 55–64.

5 Johnston, *The Christian at Play*, pp. 64–71.

6 Johnston writes: 'their functionally oriented theologies ultimately turn play into a form of work . . . [and this] aborts the world of play.' Johnston, *The Christian at Play*, p. 71.

7 Johnston, *The Christian at Play*, p. 34.

8 Johnston, *The Christian at Play*, p. 34.

9 Johnston, *The Christian at Play*, pp. 34–5.

10 Johnston, *The Christian at Play*, p. 44.

11 Johnston, *The Christian at Play*, p. 49.

12 'If we would but play, we might be surprised by the Joy of God himself. True, there is no guarantee that Joy will occur. But God has made us creatures with the capacity for communion with him, not only in and through our work

but also in and through our play. And in a time when work is proving increasingly sterile and defective, could it not be through our play that the serendipity of God's presence might most easily be experienced?' Johnston, *The Christian at Play*, p. 81.

13 Hugo Rahner, *Man at Play*, New York: Herder and Herder, 1967, pp. 11–12. Jürgen Moltmann also makes the requisite point: 'Game playing . . . corresponds to the ultimate groundlessness of the world . . . the world as free creation cannot be a necessary unfolding of God nor an emanation of his being from his divine fullness. God is free. But he does not act capriciously. When he creates something that is not God but also not nothing, then this must have its ground not in itself but in God's good will or pleasure. Hence the creation is God's play, a play of his groundless and inscrutable wisdom.' Moltmann, *Theology and Joy*, pp. 40–1.

14 Rahner, *Man at Play*, pp. 16–17. Also: 'The Aeon, however we interpret that word, is at one and the same time a king and a child, irresistible in his almighty power, and yet light-hearted and free from care as a child over his draught-board. His work is full of meaning and in this sense royal, and yet it is unnecessary and in that sense childish. It is all a divine game. It is in this dialectical paradox of king and child that expresses the metaphysical character of creation, and it is this that makes it permissible for us to speak of a playing God. So we find, not a closed cosmic system inexorably obeying its own laws, but an order directed by the Logos after the manner of a graceful game, a Logos who is separate from the created world, not identical with it. Heraclitus had grasped this truth, however dimly, and those who subsequently worked out the Logos philosophy were to make many references to the world order as a divine game.' Rahner, *Man at Play*, p. 15.

15 'Everywhere we find in such myths an intuitive feeling that the world was not created under some kind of constraint, that it did not unfold itself out of the divine in obedience to some inexorable cosmic law; rather, it was felt, was it born of a wise liberty, of the gay spontaneity of God's mind; in a word, it came from the hand of a child.' Rahner, *Man at Play*, p. 18. Rahner turns to the book of Proverbs, where Wisdom is portrayed – according to his translation – as 'a carefree child' playing before God. Rahner argues that the original word – employed twice elsewhere to describe the action of King David – has to do with a playful dance. Rahner, *Man at Play*, pp. 19–21.

16 Rahner, *Man at Play*, p. 25.

17 Rahner, *Man at Play*, p. 12.

18 Rahner, *Man at Play*, pp. 65, 87. '[I]n the last analysis there is a secret, a mystery, at the heart of every form of play, and that in it all, from the playing of children to the playing in heaven, there is one intent – the blessed seriousness of which, as Plato saw long ago, God alone is worthy. All play . . . arises from the longing for the vision of the divine; for in play all that is gay, lovely and soaring in the human spirit strives to find the expression which a man of the spirit and of enthusiasm is ever seeking to attain. There is a sacral secret at the root and in the flowering of all play . . .' Rahner, *Man at Play*, p. 65.

19 Novak also at times come perilously close to this trap. See, for example, when sport 'works' it is 'as though into the fiery heart of the Creator we had

momentary insight'. Michael Novak, *The Joy of Sports: Endzones, Bases, Baskets, Balls, and the Consecration of the American Spirit*, rev. edn, Lanham, ML: Madison, 1994, p. 159.

20 Shirl James Hoffman, *Good Game: Christianity and the Culture of Sports*, Waco, TX: Baylor University Press, 2010, p. 70.

21 Most cultures in history have confused sport with worship. The weight of empirical evidence suggests the Church – as usual – is either peculiarly right or very much wrong. As Hoffman writes: 'For ancient pagans, sports had been virtually inseparable from religious rituals. Perhaps it is better stated this way: the pagan community had sensed the rather natural way playing games could express and affirm religious realities. In standing firm against paganism, the early church defined itself not only in opposition to pagan games but also against the idea that game playing could be religious expression. As a result, the Christian community secularized sports early on, separating them from religion in a way that ancients would not have understood.' Hoffman, *Good Game*, p. 71.

22 The formal similarity between worship and sport has been widely recognized. 'We found that one of the most important characteristics of play was its spatial separation from ordinary life. A closed space is marked out for it, either materially or ideally, hedged off from the everyday surroundings. Inside this space the play proceeds, inside it the rules obtain. Now, the marking out of some sacred spot is also the primary characteristic of every sacred act. This requirement of isolation for ritual, including magic and law, is much more than merely spatial and temporal. Nearly all rites of consecration and initiation entail a certain artificial seclusion for the performers and those to be initiated . . . Sacrament and mystery presuppose a hallowed spot. Formally speaking, there is no distinction whatever between marking out a space for a sacred purpose and marking it out for the purposes of sheer play.' Huizinga, *Homo Ludens*, pp. 19–20.

23 See the *Catechism of the Catholic Church*, §§ 1136–99. Liturgy is a specific form of ritual which serves public worship in the cult. It comes from a Greek word – *leitourgia* – which denotes a public work on behalf of the people as a whole. The link between sport and liturgy has been taken up and pursued in a different direction recently by Andrew Edgar. I am indebted to Edgar for helping me sharpen my earlier accounts of sport as a ritual celebration into an account of liturgy. Edgar, however, argues that sport is a modern liturgy of despair in face of meaninglessness and completely overlooks the doctrine of creation. See Andrew Edgar, 'Sport as Liturgy: Towards a Radical Orthodoxy of Sport', *Studies in Christian Ethics* 25.1 (2012), pp. 20–34.

24 It can be argued that all Christian worship is liturgical, even the non-liturgical liturgies of some 'spontaneous' acts of worship, which are like a liturgy of spontaneity. This is clear to anyone who has experienced the repetitive nature of such 'spontaneity' in church.

25 This is because – as Sam Wells puts it – 'Worship isn't for anything. It is one of the few human activities conducted for its own sake . . . Worship has its own inner logic and intrinsic worth.' Samuel Wells, 'How Common Worship Forms Local Character', *Studies in Christian Ethics* 15.1 (2002), pp. 66–74 (cf. p. 66). Having made this point, Wells shows all the secondary benefits that result from worship.

26 The link between sport and contingency can be found in some recent literature, but – significantly – is never explained *theologically* in the way it is here. For example, Michael Novak suggests that play is 'Confidence in contingency and in Fate. Delight in creation as it is' (p. 220). 'At the heart of play is love for the finite, the limited, the bounded' (p. 232). See Novak, *Joy of Sports*.

27 The distinction between sport and worship makes this a very different theory from that of Rahner who overcomes creaturely reality *through* play, relieving us of 'all the weights . . . to be free, kingly, unfettered and divine'. Rahner, *Man at Play*, p. 65. We should note that something like the Westminster Confession states that worship is our *chief* end, not our *only* end. There is room here to find a complement to worship, not a replacement.

28 To pick up an earlier point: this reality can be described as our nature, but this nature is not un-graced. It is to say that the gift is given and that we *are* this given-ness. See Chapter 7, note 24.

29 The concept of divine freedom in relation to liturgical worship is often misunderstood. God's freedom is not simply the availability of an unlimited range of possibilities, allowing him to roam 'free', turning up spontaneously and informally wherever he wants. God's freedom is also his decision; that is, God's freedom is his commitment to life with the Church. This needs to be understood primarily through his commitment to being present in the sacraments of Eucharist and baptism. See the work of Reinhard Hütter for more on this. Reinhard Hütter, *Bound to be Free: Evangelical Catholic Engagements in Ecclesiology, Ethics and Ecumenism*, Grand Rapids, MI: Eerdmans, 2004, and *Suffering Divine Things: Theology as Church Practice*, Grand Rapids, MI: Eerdmans, 2000.

30 I am grateful to David Hilborn for helping make the connection between radical contingency, divine providence and the outcome of a game.

31 Cf. Robert W. Jenson, 'The Praying Animal', *Zygon* 18.3 (1983), pp. 311–26.

9

Exploration and Explanation: Seven Avenues for Further Thought

We have proposed that sport is a liturgy of the creature's contingency. In this chapter, we will explore the explanatory power of this proposal. I have chosen seven avenues for further thought.[1]

First, *rules*. By mapping sport onto contingency in the way we have, we get a clear idea of the value of rules in sport. As we saw in Chapter 6, the rules of any particular game are radically contingent (meaning they are in no way necessary when viewed from the outside). For example, there is no reason why a ball must bounce just once between shots in tennis or only two teams play each other in a game of football. The only reason is that these *are* the games of tennis and football. The radical contingency to the rules therefore makes these sports an appropriate way to celebrate our own contingent ordering. In effect, the contingent, internal meaning of a sport echoes the way that our own particular form – as featherless, speaking bipeds who laugh – is also internally contingent in Jesus Christ. We can therefore say: though there *are* absolutely determinative rules in both sport and creation, the rules are externally unnecessary in both. The rules in sport echo the rule of Jesus Christ. They both are freedom.

Second, *competition*. As a contest, sport will always look to produce winners *and* losers. This aspect to a game can prove difficult for Christians. Is competition really compatible with the Christian life? Is it possible to love one's neighbour while trying to beat them at baseball?[2] But under our proposal, competitive sport can be re-imagined. If sport is a liturgy of our contingency, then it requires two movements, so to speak. On one hand, the winners will face *life*, the triumphant movement out of the possibility of non-being through our obedient response to the gracious summons to exist. The losers – simultaneously – will face the nothingness from which we are summoned, the *lifelessness of non-being*. This twofold movement of winning and losing is therefore not at the expense of each other. It is instead *with* each other, because it takes both winners *and* losers to create a liturgical event in which we celebrate being invited into life out of nothing. Only together can winners and losers chime with their contingency. Only together – as *com-petitors* – can they be strung between life-with-God and nothing-with-nothingness. Sport therefore has to be competitive to be true entertainment. It is to be tensed together between winning and losing for the course of the game.[3]

That being said, because of the resurrection of Jesus Christ, Christians understand that Life is greater than death; there is no equality between the two, no eternal balance, no unending tension. Life has the final word, which is to say winning wins in the end. As a result, it will always feel much better – as we all know! – to win. Competition is no charade. Winning is better than losing. In a game, therefore, we are alive with the decision of life and death. We cheer on our team, because we do not want to die (though to know that death has been overcome, we must go to church).

Third, *idolatry*. We must recognize that there *is* something for Christians to fear in sport. This is because we do not experience sport as it is being described here. Instead, sport is corrupted, not just by the win-at-all-costs competitive realities of cheating and doping, but also by the cults of prowess, misplaced glory and shimmering celebrity. But the discrepancy between our description and our experience of sport results from the fact that reality is far more complicated than we have suggested. We have traced only the story of creation, the living event of God summoning the creature into existence to share in the eternal life of Father, Son and Spirit in Jesus Christ. But the

Church has more to say on our situation. The story of creation is supplemented by the doctrine of the Fall, the impossible possibility that the creature rejected love and instead turned away from God and neighbour, swivelling inwards and plunging headlong back towards the nothingness from which we were summoned. This falling away from our true purpose proves cataclysmic, disrupting the intricate fabric of the universe, tearing away at our existence as we seek to un-make ourselves. The consequence – as empirical evidence suggests – is completely disastrous.

In sport, the disaster takes its own particular form. Because the Fall impacts our deepest identity, our playfulness is corrupted. Instead of being non-serious, we instead take ourselves too seriously, even to the extent of deluding ourselves that we are God. As a result of this delusion, sport – in a fallen world – is no longer an expression of our most basic identity. It is also a corrupted expression of our corrupted identity.

This explains why fallen sport too easily becomes a form of idolatrous *self*-worship, nothing less than the denial of our genuine contingency by confusing ourselves with God and beginning to offer worship to ourselves. This is precisely why sport – historically as we have seen – has been bound so closely to pagan idolatry and the worship of nature. Today – though we might not want to think it – the hyped fetish of fame, celebrity, legendary status and the like is the point where sport twists and warps into a form of idolatry. Sport will always be prone to this.

We should therefore make a second (more positive) judgement about the Church's historical approach to sport. It is good that the Church has been so vigilant in its opposition to sport, because we have to recognize that sport is very bad. As a result, the Church should remain vigilant. Sport will always be a perfect arena for idolatrous self-worship. It easily slips into the pagan (self-) worship of nature.[4]

Fourth, *sport and war*. Following on from the above comments, the Christian understanding of creation and Fall should never be merged into one. Creation must instead be afforded priority. This is why the Church has refused to explain evil, instead understanding it to be in some sense absurdly parasitic on the prior good. This means that Christians recognize that the truly natural state of the creature is a state of gracious peace; it is not a state of war.[5] With this acknowledged, we can address a popular misconception of sport.

Sport is often thought to be a civilized form of war, a domesticated outlet for the pre-programmed genetic struggle for survival in the cultivated terrain of civil society. But, because the state of (original) nature is not war but peace, we can say that this way of seeing things is upside down and back to front. Of course, our fallenness means we are constantly at war with ourselves, which makes war seem primary to our twisted minds. But on a properly Christian reading of creation, war would be much better understood as a fallen state of sport rather than sport being seen as a domesticated form of war. Thus – to return to the question of competition – it is by no means self-evident that competition should be co-opted into a neo-evolutionary myth about the survival of the fittest in a brutal state of nature. This foundational metaphor need not be swallowed whole. It can instead be redeemed. Life is not a war-like struggle against each other. It is instead a competitive dance, a balletic pivoting on the edge of nothingness, spun from nothing towards eternal life. Sport simply captures this movement. It is a celebration of this contingency. It is certainly not war. War is a corruption of sport.

Fifth, *professional sport*. Our theological analysis shows that sport should not be professionalized, any more than worship should be professionalized. This is because both sport and worship are for nothing, in that nothing is harvested, nothing is produced, nothing is earned. As a result, people should not be making a living leading worship, and neither should they make a living playing sport. That said, the ideal of amateur sport will strike many as unrealistic, not least because it has been tied to all sorts of class-based injustices in the past. But idealistic though it is, the principle remains true. We need to recognize that professional sport is not true sport. It mimics it at best, it destroys it at worst. The professional sportsperson is simply an actor or a prostitute. Either way, they are not a player.[6]

That being said, how exactly we unravel the vast industry that surrounds modern sport is difficult to imagine, though there are various avenues for further exploration. It could be argued that the best approach is the current approach, that is, to pay the top professionals huge sums of money for their services. This extravagant approach has the advantage of making it unnecessary for a sportsperson to play, because they already have more money than they will really ever need. Participation – as in the days of old when only the rich could meet the amateur ideal – is in some sense unnecessary. Professional play therefore remains a free decision.

But this approach applies only to those at the very top of professional sport (where the waters are still muddied by legal contracts that would force rich professionals to play). Therefore, another approach would be to follow an old church tradition. In the church, the clergy are paid a stipend – a *living* – rather than a wage. Whether this distinction is disingenuous is up for debate, but at least it makes the point that Christian worship cannot be professionalized. Perhaps the same could apply to sports? Perhaps wages could be capped? Of course, commercial endorsements and image rights would mean that top sportspeople would still earn a fortune indirectly from the game, but at that stage their free (pseudo-amateur) decision to play would again kick in. Nonetheless, whatever approach is taken, the primary judgement remains: amateur sport is true sport; professional sport a corruption.[7]

Sixth, *gender and sport*. The corrupted nature of sport is again evidenced in the undervaluing – and denigration – of women's sport historically.[8] This can still be seen in the varying scales of remuneration today, where only two women appear in the top 100 earners in sport, an injustice that is rooted in the Victorian ideal of feminine frailty, which inevitably led to less strenuous forms of sport being created for women. Female basketball, for instance, originally involved six players to slow the game down, and golf courses today still have separate tee boxes for 'ladies'. Sport is clearly engendered. But why might this be?[9]

Numerous theories exist to explain how sport is linked to patriarchal dominance, not least in the way it provides a glorified and exalted view of a particular form of masculinity. But our theological proposal sheds new light on the matter. In a fallen society – which misreads the Genesis account of creation – women are understood to have been made *for* something; that is, the service of men. Now, if women are ontologically rationalized so to speak – in that they *are* made for something – then it follows that women are in no position to celebrate a liturgy of self-contained, meaningful non-necessity. Instead, in a fallen society, women can only ever truly chime with their being when working *for* men, at best in the kitchen or bedroom, or somewhere where they mediate the necessities of life.

On this reading, we can see that the true valuing of women's sport will only coincide with women's enjoyment of genuine equal freedoms. Until then, we will always struggle to celebrate women's sport if we do not celebrate the freedom of women. Mixed sports – such as mixed doubles in tennis – may give us a foretaste of the future. Such sports should be celebrated as a foretaste of the true end of feminism.[10]

Seventh, *good and bad sports*. The constructive proposal advanced does not have to validate all sports, though we must tread with caution here. By linking sport to our created being in the context of a fallen world, we have created some space for judging between sports. Without this space, we would be left with a difficult question: does our argument imply that there is no qualitative distinction between sports? Do we have to conclude that gladiatorial combat expresses our identity in the same way as cricket does? Or that bullfighting is as good as ice hockey?

The danger is that any judgement will involve measuring a particular sport against an external standard, which thereby appears to undermine our argument about the autotelic nature of sport. On our reading, sports must be incommensurable, in that you cannot say that table tennis is better than baseball *unless* you smuggle in some outside purpose by which to measure them both. However, autotelic does not mean autonomous. Sport – though it has a proper natural autonomy – is nested within, and accountable to, the doctrine of creation and all that means in Jesus Christ. This means that sport is not immune to analysis by theological criteria, and, on this basis, we can enquire into the merits and defects of any particular sport, examining whether it is a liturgy of our true identity as creatures in Jesus Christ.

With this in mind, we could first develop our account of the human creature further, perhaps exploring the way in which we are created as persons-in-communion, constituted not as isolated individual substances, but as relational realities. This move would allow us to underline the merits of team sports in contrast to individual pursuits, valuing basketball over sports such as weightlifting and rock climbing, for example.[11] Or we could instead decide to explore a different aspect to the human creature, thinking through the priestly form of dominion over creation and examining how this might be expressed through equine sports where two species come together in liturgical celebration. We could also make a judgement about violent sports on this basis, which – in making physical harm an end – could be identified as expressions of our fallenness rather than our truly created nature. The options are various, but the general point remains: we can give an account of better or worse sports on the basis of the extent to which they resonate with reality. That is to say, some sports *should* be more popular than others. It is because they are better attuned to who we are.

Of course, these seven points have only been sketched. Much more needs to be said on each. But these seven reflections do demonstrate the explanatory power of the theological proposal. It can help us decipher the reality of sport today, both in its popularity and its corruption, as well as enabling us to make judgements about the Church's approaches to sport in the past. But our proposal also allows us to invite Christians to approach sport differently in the future. As we have seen, the Church worked hard to decouple worship from sport. We have now recognized the propriety of this move. Worship is the liturgical celebration of who God is. Sport is the liturgical celebration of who we are. There is a world of difference between the two. But worship and sport do belong together in some sense, not least because they are both – in distinction from the necessities of life – radically *free*. We freely worship God for his intrinsic glory, just as we freely play sport to celebrate our intrinsic meaning. This freedom is the point at which they are related. Or, put otherwise, worship and sport together inform a Sabbath-shaped life.

For Christians, Sabbath is the free time that our work serves.[12] It is a set-aside time for re-creation, remaking us through the remembrance of who we are in the non-productivity of a single day. At the end of our labours, Christians gather together to sing the praises of God in Jesus Christ, who has wonderfully shared the eternal value of life in God. But – as the day of re-creation – Christians can also weave into their Sabbath the liturgy of created contingency. Sport on Sundays – like worship and rest on Sundays – enables us to resonate with our non-serious nature, reminding us that we are unimportant and invested with value only by grace and never by works. Simply put, sport complements the Sabbath-shaped liturgy of grace.[13]

That said, we would not want to get overly prescriptive about this. It is not *that* serious a matter. Christians do not *have* to play sport on Sundays. But there is a serious point that needs highlighting. Given the central claims of the doctrine of creation, Christians should be the very people who are famous – more than anyone else – for not being serious. That the opposite is the case is a travesty for which the Church bears collective responsibility. All Christians should therefore enjoy being unserious in some way or other. Sport is a great way to do it. Christians should celebrate it. Those who don't may need to repent.

Notes

1 These reflections look to meet (and move beyond) Hoffman's challenge to re-imagine sport away from the captivity of what he calls *consumer imagination* (financial and public relations), *military imaginations* (sport as battles) and *therapeutic and propaganda imaginations* (sport as tool to achieve practical ends). See Shirl James Hoffman, *Good Game: Christianity and the Culture of Sports*, Waco, TX: Baylor University Press, 2010, p. 20.

2 Shirl Hoffman's subtitle, 'Can the Mind of Christ Coexist with the Killer Instinct?' helpfully sums up the issue. Shirl J. Hoffman, 'The Sanctification of Sport', *Christianity Today* 30.6, (1986), p. 18, cited in Stuart Weir, 'Competition as Relationship: Sport as a Mutual Quest Towards Excellence', in Donald Deedorff and John White (eds), *The Image of God in the Human Body, Essays on Christianity and Sports*, New York: Edwin Mellen, 2008.

3 Sport is true *entertainment*, a word that – as Joseph L. Price has shown – denotes being held between two realities. Price uses the work of the anthropologist Victor Turner to argue that 'entertainment is a paradigmatic liminal event', tracing the etymological root of the French words *entre* and *tenir* to argue that 'the conjoined concept refer[s] to an occasion "held between". Entertainment, then, is a time that is not otherworldly but at the margins of daily life; it is a trip into a borderland area where the daily terrain can be recognized but where its contours do not determine the movement in the space "held between" it and an entirely other world.' Joseph L. Price, 'Playing and Praying, Sport and Spirit: The Forms and Functions of Prayer in Sport', *International Journal of Religion and Sport*, vol. 1 (2009), p. 77. The nature of competition – in my account – means that non-competitive sport is somewhat questionable. It also explains why close competition is better than a one-sided match. We want to live the reality of life and death *together*. This is why we love it when a game is settled only at the closing stages: a last-minute goal, a last-second touchdown.

4 By making worship a function of sport, ancient cultures demonstrate their unredeemed nature. Interestingly, given the Fall and redemption, Hoffmann attempts to re-imagine the 'killer instinct' of competition away from the corrupted norms, which he sees as distortions of relationship (pp. 145–65). Can we not imagine a redeemed game, he asks? Why not make it 'Grace' *with* 'Humility' rather than 'First Baptists' *against* 'First Methodists'? Hoffman, *Good Game*, p. 289.

5 See the important work of John Milbank who argues the primacy of peace not war. John Milbank, *Theology and Social Theory: Beyond Secular Reason*, Oxford: Blackwell, 1990.

6 'As for the professionals – the boxers, cyclists, jockeys, or actors who earn their living in the ring, track or hippodrome or on the stage, and who must think in terms of prize, salary, or title – it is clear that they are not players but workers. When they play, it is at some other game.' Roger Caillois, *Man, Play and Games*, Urbana and Chicago, IL: University of Illinois Press, 2001, p. 6.

7 There is an analogy to be made here between sport and sex. Sex should not be professionalized, either as porn or prostitution. As a friend of mine

commented, given my argument, my ongoing attendance at Arsenal is the equivalent of me watching pornography and should therefore cease. I am still trying to work out the right answer to this quandary!

8 For a summary of the issues, see Nancy Theberge, 'Gender and Sport', in Jay Coakley and Eric Dunning (eds), *Handbook of Sports Studies*, London: Sage Publications, 2002, pp. 322–33.

9 Theberge, 'Gender and Sport', p. 323. Alternatively, other sports such as ice hockey were deemed to be solely the preserve of men until very recently. For earnings, see Forbes list at http://www.forbes.com/sites/kurtbadenhausen/ 2011/05/31/the-worlds-highest-paid-athletes/.

10 This would not rule out separate sports for men and women, or competitions between the two. Sexual difference is to be properly celebrated, not brutally overcome.

11 It is at least questionable whether rock climbing is an individual sport given that most climbers will be depending on their partners to hold the rope. The point remains, however.

12 See discussion on the 'rest of Sabbath' in Robert K. Johnston, *The Christian at Play*, Grand Rapids, MI: Eerdmans, 1997, pp. 88–95.

13 There is still much opposition to sport on Sundays in the Church. See the regular call for non-sporting Sundays in Kevin Lixey, Christoph Hübenthal, Dietmar Mieth and Norbert Müller (eds), *Sport and Christianity: A Sign of the Times in the Light of Faith*, Washington: Catholic University of America Press, 2012.

10

Concluding Comments:
Christians and Sport Today

Thinking through the question of sport has helped me appreciate why I love football so much. It has helped me see football for what it is. It is a chance for me to bounce up against my meaningful non-necessity. Nowadays, therefore, when I go to a game, I can understand why it is an endless round of delight and anxiety. I can understand why we must swing between hope and despair, joy and desolation, life and nothingness, because our being is somehow compressed into those 90 minutes, strung across a pitch, suspended above an abyss. Football, I love it.

Of course, I've become acutely aware of the dangers in sport: the irresistible slide towards hostility and violence, the stench of greed and win-at-all-costs cheating, the corruption of fame and the creep of commercialism. When I do chime with my being, it is amid the discordant noise of a corrupted reality, my own included.[1]

The day after a match, I usually make my way to church. There another crowd gathers. We also get caught up in the flow of a drama, singing and embracing, as we worship Jesus Christ in the liturgical movement of the Eucharist. Just as with Arsenal, there is no justification for it, no rationale for it, no purpose beyond the immediate event itself in which we never make anything, produce anything, and serve no tangible purpose. Our worship – like our sport – is an end in itself, a gratuitous celebration of life.[2]

Yet, things in church are very different from things in sport. In church, we face outwards, travelling together towards the very edges of our being and gazing out beyond ourselves into Life himself (who we find is heading back our way, from every direction). Here we are not facing inwards, not chiming with our own being. Instead, we bounce up against the One who loves in freedom, the meaning of our life, Jesus Christ with his people. This is why Christians should never confuse sport with worship. They are fundamentally different directions, different ways in being.

This is much easier said than done, however. There really is a quasi-religious aura surrounding sport today.[3] Be it the Super Bowl, the World Cup, the World Series or at Arsenal, sporting events are awash with religious symbol and meaning. Many sociologists now underline the link between modern sport and religion.[4] They see how participants are given a way to describe the world ('life is a game'). They see that they are affirmed in basic values ('sportsmanship', 'being a good loser'). More imaginatively still, some even link governing bodies to patriarchs and councils, the modern media acting like scribes, penning their fables about iconic trophies, the stadiums like temples, the devoted fans, the worshipped stars.[5] False though it is, sport still works like a religion today.[6]

However, there are other sociologists who argue that contemporary sport is not religious.[7] There is no transcendental element in it, no sacramental aspect to it. It is instead defined by the secular values of equality, rationalization, specialization, bureaucracy, quantified achievement and record keeping, none of which – they argue – are at all religious.[8] But even if sport and religion are fundamentally different, they still compete today for money, time, perhaps even souls. Whichever way we look at it, religion and sport are still closely connected.[9]

Christians therefore need to remain vigilant. Sport's corruption runs deep. It lends itself so easily to an idolatrous agenda in which we imagine ourselves – in one way or another – to be worthy of our worship. Christians should therefore continue to think through the question of sport, debating whether we should be paying to watch professionals or join in with events like the Olympics, all of which is to raise the age-old (tricky) question of how Christians are to be in the world, not of it.

Over recent decades, however, we have witnessed the rise of sport chaplaincies and ministries, as well as evangelistic programmes targeted especially at sport. Sports evangelism is big in the USA, where the unquestioned popularity of sports seems to fuel a desire to treat it as a mission field.[10] It is of course entirely natural (or, ideally, supernatural) for Christians to tell their friends about Jesus, and this will apply to Christians in sport just as much as anywhere else. But we must be careful. Sport can be spoilt.

There is therefore a question mark over the way Christians play hard *and* witness hard. Is it right for a victorious athlete to bear witness to God through a T-shirt or a post-game interview that is littered with praise? One commentator has called this new phenomenon 'sportianity': just as a sporting hero is a marketing dream for businesses, so too a successful sportsperson is the best advert for the gospel.[11] But as with idolatrous self-importance, instrumental use of sport to the 'glory of God' should be resisted. Christians should simply play sport for sport, not for the opportunities it presents, be they health, wealth or evangelistic stage. With sport, these things are secondary.

Instead, the task for Christians is to commentate on sport. We can help people understand why it is so popular. We can explain what is so great about it. We can point out to its fans – whether in stadiums, parks, arenas or back gardens – that they are enjoying a liturgy of contingency, a wonderfully unnecessary but internally meaningful way to chime with their own unnecessary but meaningful life as creatures of God. That is why we love sport. And that is little known.

Of course, all this depends on whether the argument here is correct. We must again recognize that the constructive argument is only a proposal. We are nowhere near speaking the final word on the subject. Instead, we are hopefully igniting a debate, encouraging Christians to think through the question of sport in light of the good news of Jesus Christ.

There is evidently a need for this, as many commentators have recognized.[12] Our constructive proposal therefore places a marker in the sand. Other Christians can measure it, develop it or radically revise it, but the hope is that they won't ignore it, because – whatever its merits – the argument is written in the belief that sport is an immovable feature in human life. It is about our deepest identity. It is to resonate with our own contingency.[13]

And that contingency will never end. In Jesus Christ, we will always be creatures. And just so: though the heavenly city may have no temple, Christians can be confident that it will have a stadium where we can continue to chime. Sport is here to stay. We can enjoy it for ever.[14]

Notes

1 There are few places in life as good as a football crowd in which to discover the good and bad in the human creature. The crowd is like our subconscious: a source of gross darkness and also a source of great humour and creativity. Darkness and light often come together in the songs and chants, especially when they are directed at the opposition players and manager (and also their mothers).

2 The dangers of Sunday school and children's church with its productivity should be noted here. Recent popes have been keen to stress the educational value of sport for young people, refusing to let it stand alone but instead harnessing it to an agenda of improvement. For example, Pope Benedict XVI: 'Of course, an after-school centre where only games were played and refreshments provided would be absolutely superfluous. The point of an after-school catechetical and recreation centre must be cultural, human and Christian formation for a mature personality.' On our reading, such instrumentalization is a corruption of sport. See Josef Clemens, 'Sport in the Magisterium of Benedict XVI', in Kevin Lixey, Christoph Hübenthal, Dietmar Mieth and Norbert Müller (eds), *Sport and Christianity: A Sign of the Times in the Light of Faith*, Washington: Catholic University of America Press, 2012, p. 152.

3 See Joseph L. Price, 'An American Apotheosis: Sports as Popular Religion', in Bruce David Forbes and Jeffery H. Mahan (eds), *Religion and Popular Culture in America*, Berkeley, CA: University of California Press, 2000, pp. 201–18.

4 Again, see Price, 'American Apotheosis', pp. 201–18. See also Steven J. Overman, *The Protestant Ethic and the Spirit of Sport: How Calvinism and Capitalism Shaped America's Games*, Macon, GA: Mercer University Press, 2011, pp. 9ff.

5 Cf. Price, 'American Apotheosis'.

6 Even if it is not a religion, it can function as a 'functional equivalent of religion'. Overman, *Protestant Ethic and the Spirit of Sport*, p. 9.

7 E.g. Harry Edwards, Edwin Cady, Joan Chandler and Robert J. Higgs. See Price, 'American Apotheosis'.

8 Recent research into the phenomenon of *flow* seriously questions this conclusion from a secular direction. Flow is the zen-like state of optimal focus in the present. The player is totally absorbed into the activity. See the work of Csikszentmihalyi in this field, e. g. Susan A. Jackson and Mihaly Csikszentmihalyi, *Flow in Sports*, Champaign, IL: Human Kinetics, 1999. See also, Overman, *Protestant Ethic and the Spirit of Sport*, p. 11.

9 'Sport owns Sunday now', as one commentator put it. And more money is spent on the Super Bowl than is given in a month to religious institutions. Price, 'American Apotheosis', pp. 201–4.

10 Dominic Erdozain, 'In Praise of Folly: Sport as Play', *Anvil* 28.1 (2012).

11 Hoffman offers a wonderful description of *sportianity* in Shirl James Hoffman, *Good Game: Christianity and the Culture of Sports*, Waco, TX: Baylor University Press, 2010, pp. 13–15.

12 Shirl Hoffman is right to conclude that sport is 'a topic neglected by Christian intellectuals'. Hoffman, *Good Game*, p. 20. Anderson and Marino also note how 'Despite the long co-evolution of sport and religion, there have been few academic venues open to the discussion of their intricate interrelationship.' Christopher J. Anderson and Gordon Marino (eds), *International Journal of Religion and Sport* 1 (2009), editors' page.

13 To put the point in the terms of the argument: this constructive work is, in some sense, not that serious. In fact, in its provocative and questionable form, it is itself almost playful. In other words, I do not hold tightly to every aspect of it, though I believe that the reality of sport is as it has been presented here.

14 See Revelation 21.22.

Bibliography

Anderson, Christopher J. and Gordon Marino (eds), *International Journal of Religion and Sport* 1 (2009).

Barber, Richard and Juliet Barker, *Tournaments: Jousts, Chivalry and Pageants in the Middle Ages* (Woodbridge: Boydell Press, 2000).

Baker, William Joseph, *Playing with God: Religion and Modern Sport* (Cambridge, MA: Harvard University Press, 2007).

Barnes, Simon, *The Meaning of Sport* (London: Short Books, 2006).

Barth, Karl, *Dogmatics in Outline* (London: SCM Press, 1949).

—— *Wolfgang Amadeus Mozart* (Eugene, OR: Wipf and Stock, 2003).

Bernstein, Richard J., *Beyond Objectivism and Relativism: Science, Hermeneutics, and Praxis* (Oxford: Basil Blackwell, 1983).

Bickley, Paul and Sam Tomlin, *Give us our Ball Back: Reclaiming Sport for the Common Good* (London: Theos, 2012).

Brown, Peter, *Through the Eye of a Needle: Wealth, the Fall of Rome and the Making of Christianity in the West, 350–550 AD* (Princeton, NJ: Princeton University Press, 2012).

Caillois, Roger, *Man, Play and Games*, trans. Meyer Barash (Urbana and Chicago, IL: University of Illinois Press, 2001).

Carcopino, Jerome, *Daily Life in Ancient Rome: The People and the City at the Height of the Empire* (Harmondsworth: Penguin, 1991; Kindle edition, 2008).

Chester, Tim, *Delighting in the Trinity* (Grand Rapids, MI and Oxford: Monarch Books, 2005).

Coleman, K. M., 'Fatal Charades: Roman Executions Staged as Mythological Enactments', *Journal of Roman Studies* 80 (1990), pp. 44–70.

Conner, Steven, *A Philosophy of Sport* (London: Reaktion Books, 2011).

Craig, Steve, *Sports and Games of the Ancients* (Westport, CT: Greenwood Press, 2002).

Crouch, David, *Tournament* (London and New York: Hambledon and Continuum, 2005).

—— *The Image of Aristocracy in Britain: 1000–1300* (London: Routledge, 1992).

Culin, Stewart, *Games of the North American Indians* (New York: Dover Publications, 1975).

Dickie, Matthew W., 'Fair and Foul Play in the Funeral Games in the Iliad', *Journal of Sport History* 11.2 (1984), pp. 8–17.

Edgar, Andrew, 'Sport as Liturgy: Towards a Radical Orthodoxy of Sport', *Studies in Christian Ethics* 25.1 (2012), pp. 20–34.

Erdozain, Dominic, *The Problem of Pleasure: Sport, Recreation and the Crisis of Victorian Religion* (Woodbridge: Boydell, 2010).

—— 'In Praise of Folly: Sport as Play', *Anvil* 28.1 (2012), pp. 20–34.

Fergusson, David A. S., *The Cosmos and the Creator: An Introduction to the Theology of Creation* (London: SPCK, 1998).

Fergusson, Erna, *Dancing Gods: Indian Ceremonials of New Mexico and Arizona* (New York: Alfred A. Knopf, 1931).

Foster, Michael, 'The Christian Doctrine of Creation and the Rise of Modern Science', *Mind* 43 (1934), pp. 446–68.

Gunton, Colin E., *The Triune Creator: A Historical and Systematic Study* (Grand Rapids, MI: Eerdmans, 1998).

—— *The Promise of Trinitarian Theology* (2nd edn, London and New York: T & T Clark, 2003).

Guttmann, Allen, *Sports: The First Five Millennia* (Amherst and Boston, MA: University of Massachusetts Press, 2004).

Hefele, Charles Joseph, *A History of the Christian Councils from the Original Documents* (2nd edn, 1.3.15. London: T & T Clark, 1883).

Heinegg, Peter, 'Philosophy of Football', *Christian Century* 91.43 (1974), p. 1198.

Higgs, Robert J. and Michael C. Braswell, *An Unholy Alliance: The Sacred and Modern Sport* (Macon, GA: Mercer University Press, 2004).

Hoffman, Shirl James, *Good Game: Christianity and the Culture of Sports* (Waco, TX: Baylor University Press, 2010).

Holmes, Stephen R., *The Holy Trinity: Understanding God's Life* (Milton Keynes: Paternoster, 2012).

Huizinga, Johan, *Homo Ludens: A Study of the Play Element in Culture* (Boston, MA: Beacon Press, 1955).

Hütter, Reinhard, *Suffering Divine Things: Theology as Church Practice* (Grand Rapids, MI: Eerdmans, 2000).

—— *Bound to be Free: Evangelical Catholic Engagements in Ecclesiology, Ethics and Ecumenism* (Grand Rapids, MI: Eerdmans, 2004).

Hyland, Drew, *A Philosophy of Sport* (Lanham, MD: University Press of America, 1990).

Jackson, Susan A. and Mihaly Csikszentmihalyi, *Flow in Sports* (Champaign, IL: Human Kinetics, 1999).

Jenson, Robert W., 'The Praying Animal', *Zygon* 18.3 (1983), pp. 311–26.

—— *Systematic Theology*, vol. 1, *The Triune God* (New York and Oxford: Oxford University Press, 1997).

—— *Systematic Theology*, vol. 2, *The Works of God* (New York and Oxford: Oxford University Press, 1999).

—— *The Triune Identity: God According to the Gospel* (Eugene, OR: Wipf and Stock, 2002).

—— *On Thinking the Human: Resolutions of Difficult Notions* (Grand Rapids, MI and Cambridge: Eerdmans, 2003).

—— 'Christ as Culture 2: Christ as Art', *International Journal of Systematic Theology* 6.1 (2004), pp. 69–76.

Johnston, Robert K., *The Christian at Play* (Grand Rapids, MI: Eerdmans, 1997).

Kaeuper, Richard, *Chivalry and Violence in Medieval Europe* (new edn, Oxford: Oxford University Press, 2001).

—— *Holy Warriors: The Religious Ideology of Chivalry* (Philadelphia, PA: University of Pennsylvania Press, 2009).

Keen, Maurice, *Chivalry* (New Haven, CT and London: Yale University Press, 2005).

Kelly, Christopher, *The Roman Empire: A Very Short Introduction* (Oxford: Oxford University Press, 2006).

Kelner, Martin, *Sit Down and Cheer: A History of Sport on TV* (Guildford: John Wisden and Company, 2012).

Kluck, Ted, *The Reason for Sports: A Christian Fanifesto* (Chicago, IL: Moody Publishers, 2009).

Köhne, Eckart, 'Bread and Circuses: the Politics of Entertainment', in Eckart Köhne, Cornelia Ewigleben and Ralph Jackson (eds), *Gladiators and Caesars: The Power of the Spectacle in Ancient Rome* (Berkeley and Los Angeles: University of California Press, 2000), pp. 8–30.

Laderman, Gary and Luis D. León, *Religion and American Cultures: An Encyclopaedia of Traditions*, vol. 1 (Santa Barbara, CA: ABC-CLIO Reference Publishers, 2003).

Lixey, Kevin, Christoph Hübenthal, Dietmar Mieth and Norbert Müller (eds), *Sport and Christianity: A Sign of the Times in the Light of Faith* (Washington: Catholic University of America Press, 2012).

Lixey, Kevin, Norbert Müller and Cornelius Schafer (eds), *Blessed John Paul II Speaks to Athletes: Homilies, Messages and Speeches on Sport* (London: John Paul II Sports Foundation, 2012).

Lupson, Peter, *Thank God for Football: The Illustrated Companion* (London: SPCK, 2010).

Marsden, George M., *The Outrageous Idea of Christian Scholarship* (Oxford and New York: Oxford University Press, 1997).

Mason, Bryan, *The Teaching of Physical Education: A Biblical Perspective* (The Christian Institute, 2002), available at http://www.christian.org.uk/html-publications/education9.htm.

Milbank, John, *Theology and Social Theory: Beyond Secular Reason* (Oxford: Blackwell, 1990).

Moltmann, Jürgen, *Theology and Joy* (London: SCM Press, 1973).

Novak, Michael, *The Joy of Sports: Endzones, Bases, Baskets, Balls, and the Consecration of the American Spirit* (rev. edn, Lanham, ML: Madison, 1994).

Nuechterlein, James, 'The Wide World of Sports', *First Things* 49 (1995), pp. 8–9.

Opler, Morris Edward, 'The Jicarilla Apache Ceremonial Relay Race', *American Anthropologist* 46.1 (1944), pp. 75–97.

Orwell, George, 'The Sporting Spirit', *Tribune* (14 December 1945).

Overman, Steven J., *The Protestant Ethic and the Spirit of Sport: How Calvinism and Capitalism Shaped America's Games* (Macon, GA: Mercer University Press, 2011).

Pieper, Josef, *Leisure: The Basis of Culture*, trans. Gerald Malsbary (South Bend, IN: St Augustine's Press, 1998).

Potter, David, *The Victor's Crown: A History of Ancient Sport from Homer to Byzantium* (London: Quercus, 2011).

Placher, William C., *Unapologetic Theology: A Christian Voice in a Pluralist Conversation* (Louisville, KY: Westminster John Knox Press, 1989).

Polley, Martin (ed.), *The History of Sport in Britain, 1880–1914* (London: Routledge, 2003).

Price, Joseph L., 'An American Apotheosis: Sports as Popular Religion', in Bruce David Forbes and Jeffery H. Mahan (eds), *Religion and Popular Culture in America* (Berkeley, CA: University of California Press, 2000), pp. 201–18.

—— 'Playing and Praying, Sport and Spirit: The Forms and Functions of Prayer in Sport', *International Journal of Religion and Sport*, vol. 1 (2009), pp. 55–80.

Rahner, Hugo, *Man at Play* (New York: Herder and Herder, 1967).

Reeves, Michael, *The Good God: Enjoying Father, Son and Spirit* (Milton Keynes: Paternoster, 2012).

Riley-Smith, Jonathan, *The Crusades, Christianity and Islam* (New York: University of Columbia Press, 2008).

Riordan, James, 'Soviet-style Sport in Eastern Europe: The End of an Era', in Lincoln Allison (ed.), *The Changing Politics of Sport* (Manchester: Manchester University Press, 1993).

—— 'The Impact of Communism on Sport', *Historical Social Research* 32.1 (2007), pp. 110–15.

Rock, Tom, 'More than a Game', *Lacrosse Magazine* (November/December 2002), available at http://redhawkslax.com/articles/152-more-than-a-game-lacrosse-at-the-onondaga-nation-connects-the-current-generation-with-its-ancestors.

Sapra, Rahul, 'Sports in India', in Dale Hoiberg and Indu Ramchandani (eds), *Students' Britannica India: Select Essays* (New Delhi: Britannica, 2000).

Smith, Ed, *What Sport Tells Us about Life* (London: Penguin, 2009).

Speer, Albert, *Inside the Third Reich* (New York: Simon & Schuster, 1997).

Spivey, Nigel, *The Ancient Olympics* (2nd edn, Oxford: Oxford University Press, 2012).

Struna, Nancy, 'Puritans and Sport: The Irretrievable Tide of Change', *Journal of Sport History* 4.1 (1977), pp. 1–21.

Theberge, Nancy, 'Gender and Sport', in Jay Coakley and Eric Dunning (eds), *Handbook of Sports Studies* (London: Sage, 2002), pp. 322–33.

Toulmin, Stephen, *Cosmopolis: The Hidden Agenda of Modernity* (Chicago, IL: University of Chicago Press, 1992).

Vander Zwaag, H. J., *Toward a Philosophy of Sport* (Fort Worth, TX: University of Texas Press, 1985).

Watson, Nick, 'Book Review: *An Unholy Alliance: The Sacred and Modern Sports* by Robert J. Higgs and Michael C. Braswell, 2004', *Implicit Religion* 10.3 (2007), pp. 314–16.

Watson, Nick J. and Daniel R. Czech, 'The Use of Prayer in Sport: Implications for Sport Psychology Consulting', *Athletic Insight* 7.4 (2005), pp. 26–35.

Watson, Nick J. and Andrew Parker (eds), *Sports and Christianity: Historical Contemporary Perspectives* (New York and Abingdon: Routledge, 2013).

Weir, Stuart, 'Competition as Relationship: Sport as a Mutual Quest towards Excellence', in Donald Deedorff and John White (eds), *The Image of God in the Human Body, Essays on Christianity and Sports* (New York: Edwin Mellen, 2008), pp. 93–114.

Wells, Samuel, 'How Common Worship Forms Local Character', *Studies in Christian Ethics* 15.1 (2002), pp. 66–74.

Whannel, Garry, 'Sport and the Media', in Jay Coakley and Eric Dunning (eds), *Handbook of Sports Studies* (London: Sage, 2002), p. 293.

Wiedemann, Thomas, *Emperors and Gladiators* (London and New York: Routledge, 1992).

Wilcox, Pete, 'Glory', in Samuel Wells and Sarah Coakley (eds), *Praying for England: Priestly Presence in Contemporary Culture* (London and New York: Continuum, 2008), pp. 41–64.

Williams, Rowan, *Not Being Serious: Thomas Merton and Karl Barth* (2008), available at http://rowanwilliams.archbishopofcanterbury.org/articles.php/1205/not-being-serious-thomas-merton-and-karl-barth.

Young, Frances, '"Creatio Ex Nihilo": A Context for the Emergence of the Christian Doctrine of Creation', *Scottish Journal of Theology*, vol. 44 (1991), pp. 139–52.

Index of Biblical Citations

Index of Names and Subjects

Lightning Source UK Ltd.
Milton Keynes UK
UKHW010100121218
333832UK00003B/155/P